Questions

I know I didn't grow inside you,
I know you said I grew in your heart.
I know you wanted me more then anything,
adopted meant loved, right from the start.

I have a question for you Mummy,
now that I am five years old.
Does adoption make me different?
Can we talk about what I've been told?

Adoption means someone loves you,
adoption gave my forever home.
It gave me a place to run to,
so I would never feel alone.

I have a question for you Mummy,
now that I am almost a teen.
Adoption does make me feel different,
learning some people can be so mean.

I don't know where I came from,
I don't know where I belong.
How can I handle all of these questions?
It's hard to always be strong.

I have a question for you Mummy,
will you come and hold my hand?
Now that the day has come to meet her,
I need to understand.

Now I know where it all started,
adopted meant loved, right from the start.
She loved me enough to give me away,
but in her heart we were never apart.

The day I became a mummy,
that day, just my son and I.
He gave me a love to be strong for,
learning a mother's love would never die.

I have a question for you Daddy,
now that I'm five years old.
Does adoption like mummy make me different?
Can we talk about what I've been told?

by Aoife Curran

Introduction

I grew up in Rathfarnham in Dublin, in a small cul-de-sac where everyone knew everyone and there was always a neighbour or a friend you could call into for a cuppa. My parents adopted me when I was 10 weeks old into an amazing, kind and inspiring family. I have a brother called Carl who is also adopted and is two years older than me – my partner in crime. I couldn't tell you where my parents got their understanding, strength and security from, but adoption was always a word that was used so freely in our house. Ever since I could talk and ask questions, they would speak to me about it and listen to me, trying as best they could to answer my many questions. Although Carl and I were very close we were very different and we both looked at being adopted in a very different way. My parents knew this and they knew I felt like I needed to speak about it a lot more than he did so they made sure to accommodate that.

This turned out to be such an important factor in my life as it helped me to gain the same sense of importance in honesty, which was essential when I had my own son later in life and was again confronted with the adoption process. So in those early years, adoption was a very positive thing in my life. To me it meant that somebody loved me very much and that's down to my parents who had an amazing way of helping me to focus on that, rather than on what could have been. At times it was a painful realisation that somebody else gave me away but my mum, even though we don't always see eye-to-eye just like any mother and daughter, has been my inspiration. Without even knowing it, she has been my mum, my best friend (sometimes my worst enemy while a teenager – although that never lasted for long), my counsellor, my crutch and not only grandmother, but another mother to my children too when I wasn't strong enough. She taught me the difference between right and wrong and how important honesty was with the things in life that are not always easy to be honest about.

A relative of hers was adopted and he was never told as a child. He eventually found out during an argument with his own father when he was 18 years old and so she was never going to let that happen to us. It is because of how she dealt with my adoption and me as a child that I knew how to deal with the adoption of my own son, when my husband was adopting him.

Where do I start telling you about my dad? I have always been and I'm sure always will be a daddy's girl. When I was small and I hurt myself, when I was older and got in trouble, even when my friends and I discovered nightclubs and needed a lift home at 3am, my dad was always there. He still is. My security blanket, my closest friend, always understanding, never judgemental – even when I tested him to the limit! No matter what I went on to learn through my journey, the one thing that I knew right from the very start, that nobody needed to teach me, was that my mum and dad were always and will always be my mum and dad. Nobody else could ever fill their shoes.

My brother Carl, what a great guy! He has grown up to be a man that any mother would be proud of and as his sister I am immensely proud of him too. He is the kind of person that everyone always wants to be around and he is always there if you need a shoulder to cry on. We were always very close growing up. We had our fights like every brother and sister but he has always been there for me, through thick and thin and I will always be there for him. Over the years he never seemed to be as interested as me in the fact that he was adopted, or maybe it's just that boys and girls are different? But just like me, he was very happy in the family he became a part of and for all of the special memories from my childhood he was right there by my side.

I could not write a book about my life without telling you about my three best friends. They have been the centre of my universe forever and I was very lucky throughout my childhood, and as an adult, to have them. We all lived within a few houses of each other on our little cul-de-sac and have been through everything together. Through thick and thin, good times and bad, it has always been Clare, Katherine, Amy and I. Thick as thieves, we are more like sisters than friends. The girls have been my support system and have been there for me in every way. I would not have got through any of the hard times in my life without them. So many of the good times in my life were so special because of them too.

Because of the deep love and respect that I have for my family and friends I believe that it is impossible to portray a true reflection of my story without involving them to a certain degree and so when I finished writing this book, not only did I pass it to them to see what they thought – I invited them to be a part of it. So each of my closest allies, my family, my girls, my husband and my eldest son, Jack, have all voiced their opinions at some stage within these pages. After all adoption isn't about one person, it's about the parents, both birth and adoptive, the brothers and sisters – the ones you grow up with and the ones you discover. It's about your childhood friends and the ones you make along the way. It's about their families and it's about the family you build for yourself – your spouse and your own children – whether they are adopted or not.

This is a story of laughter and of tears, of journeys taken with both positive and negative outcomes. It's about learning, growing and understanding that in order to cope with your adoption you must respect the parties involved and try to come to terms with their reasoning before you decide how you feel about what's happened. *Searching For Me* is just one person's journey, mine, but it is one filled with determination and hope – two attributes that I never let go of and in the end never let me down.

I hope this book can help support you throughout your adoption journey, or enlighten you if you are simply reading out of curiosity, because writing it has helped me throughout mine and for that alone it has been worth every second.

About the Author

Aoife is a 31-year-old mother of three from Dublin, now living in Kildare. All of her life she has known that she is adopted, but she could never have imagined the ups and downs she would face when finding her birth parents.

Hers is a beautiful story of a girl filled with admiration and respect for the wonderful couple she has called Mum and Dad for as long as she can remember. A girl who also showed unimaginable insight and maturity when confronting her birth parents and understanding their decisions – the ones that shaped the rest of her life.

In telling her story Aoife is a breath of fresh air and *'Searching For Me - My Adoption Story,'* is sure to help those in similar situations as well as enlighten those for whom adoption was never, and never will be, an issue.

Dedication

Dedicated to my parents, for never letting go of my hand.
This book is for you. X

Searching For Me

My Adoption Story

by
Aoife Curran

December 2013

Searching For Me – My Adoption Story

2013

Published by Emu Ink Ltd
www.emuink.ie

Cover design by Gwen Taylour

ISBN: 978-1-909684-26-3

Acknowledgements

Thank you doesn't seem enough to say to my parents. You are the reason I am the person I turned out to be. I was meant to be your child and you were meant to be my parents.

Searching For Me would never have been written if it wasn't for my husband Daniel. Thank you from the bottom of my heart for inspiring me and making me strive to be the best possible version of myself. By following in your footsteps you have shown me, through hard work and determination, that dreams can come true. I love you.

To my three beautiful children Jack, Jessica and Grace, I love you all so much, you are my reason for everything. Thank you for being my teachers.

Apart from friends and loved ones mentioned in my book there is one other person who deserves a huge thank you. Whether I need a friend or an extra pair of eyes for editing or even just a chat and a coffee, one of my closest friends Niamh Lanigan is always there. You have no idea the impact your presence has in my life.

And finally, none of this would have been possible without the help and support of Emer Cleary at Emu Ink. You gave me confidence to tell my story and put in so much work to help me make publishing it a reality.

March 2nd 1982

Dear Mr and Mrs M,

This is just a note to confirm that our committee has accepted your adoption application for your second baby and your
name is now on our waiting list. We hope we do not have to
keep you waiting too long.

With all good wishes,
Yours sincerely,
Sarah (Adoption worker)

April 16th 1982

Dear Mr and Mrs M,

I thought I should put this in writing rather than phoning you
and taking you by surprise.
We have now chosen your baby daughter, born on the 10th
February and she is available for you just as soon as you can
take her. She is a lovely blonde baby weighing 3.20kg at birth
and she has had her six-week check. I will of course give you
more information about her and her background when I am
talking to you.
I would in fact like to place her with you on Friday afternoon
next April 23rd. I could have her here for you at 4.30pm.
Perhaps you would ring me as soon as you get this letter.

With kind wishes,
Yours sincerely,
Sarah (Adoption worker)

This was to be the start of the journey towards my life with my new family. It was however the end of my parents' journey to have children – a journey that had begun some years before.

I believe that everything happens for a reason and there are so many bits and pieces throughout my life that could be put down to amazing coincidence, but I strongly put it down to fate! If you are of the same thinking, read on, and if you're not, well read on anyway, I'd like to try to convince you…

Chapter 1 – Adoption, baby steps

MY parents met on December 24th, 1977 at a Christmas Eve mass and what followed was a bit of a whirlwind romance. Mum was 37 and dad was 35. They both had good jobs and had already (separately) done a lot of travelling. By June the following year they had got engaged and by that September 24th they were married. They had both always wanted to have children, but unfortunately things were not to be that straightforward for them. By 1980 when they still had no luck, they had decided that it was time to have some fertility tests.

On the May 22nd, a date that in time would become a very significant one in their lives, they had an appointment in Holles Street hospital to receive their fertility test results. They walked around Merrion Square and down to Holles Street, knowing that what they were about to find out, either way, was something that would change their lives forever. Dad was keeping pace with the busy people around them in shirts and skirts hurrying to enjoy their lunch break in the park on what was a beautiful summer's day, when he noticed mum was slightly lagging behind.

"Are you OK love?"

"Mac, we have been waiting for this day for so long and now that it is here I don't feel ready to go in," my mum said nervously.

"I know how you feel my love, but we can't think like that now. We will be fine and I am sure our tests will come back clear. We have come so far already, the sun is shining and it is a beautiful day to celebrate."

"You're right and sure look, even if they do find something wrong I am sure it won't be big and they can just fix it and there will be nothing left to stop us from having our baby."

Both of them decided to project positivity, trying to stop the fear that was lurking somewhere in the pit of their stomachs, from creeping in. They decided to focus on the positives and support each other, on the outside anyway.

As they sat waiting in the corridor for the doctor every scenario ran through their minds. Watching all the pregnant women walking past them on their way to their appointments and the new mothers and fathers leaving the hospital for the first time with their new babies they looked at themselves, no bump, no baby – just fear.

Their thoughts were eventually interrupted by a door creaking open beside them and a smiling, smartly dressed, older man in a grey suit beckoning them over.

"Mr and Mrs Mc Namara, would you both like to take a seat inside my office?"

For what felt like an eternity, they sat in his office watching him slowly walk across the room and sit down without saying another word. As he began to arrange all the files on his desk, eventually coming across theirs, he stared intently at each page. Dad tried to busy himself by reading all of the plaques on the wall. He could not even bring himself to make small talk with his wife, whose insides were screaming as loudly as his.

The doctor eventually spoke.

"As you know, we have completed a number of tests, due to the fact that you were having issues conceiving, and unfortunately these tests have brought us to the conclusion that it is not possible for you to have children. I understand this is far from the news you were hoping for but I am here to answer any questions that either of you may have."

In that split second it felt like all of the oxygen had been sucked out of the room. Dad was the first to find his words as he attempted to comfort my mother who was sobbing quietly into her hands.

"Its OK love, please don't cry," he said as he cradled her hands in his. "Doctor, how accurate are these tests? Is there any point in getting a second opinion? I mean everybody makes mistakes sometimes and this could be one of those times. We are good people, we eat right, we don't drink or smoke... I don't understand. Why us?" His eyes were misting over despite himself.

"I understand you will have a lot of questions but rest assured Mr and Mrs Mc Namara, we have exhausted all of the tests available to us and I am very sorry to say that there is nothing we, or anyone else, can do to change the outcome here."

With his tears now flowing freely my dad, determined even in that moment, turned to my devastated mother and said, "One way or another we will have children." And with that he handed her a tissue.

The doctor picked up on dad's strength of character and added, "There is so much for you both to take in here today and you will need time for it to sink in, of course, but Mrs Mc Namara your husband is right. This by no means has to be the end of your dreams to have children. There are many things to consider here. Have you ever thought about adoption?"

For the first time since entering the office mum lifted her head, encouraged, and said, "Well, we were afraid this would happen so, yes, we have already started the process."

"Great, then you are a step ahead already."

It was just what they needed to give them the strength to stand up, thank the doctor for his time and patience and open the door to face the world again, passing all of the bumps and babies on the way – their own hearts broken in two.

Little did they know, however, that on that very day in Holles Street hospital, where they were receiving their devastating news, there was a little boy, with a big mop of brown hair, being born on the floor above them.
In 10 short weeks, that little boy would become their son.

*

At that time in Ireland, adoption was fairly common. Even on my mum and dad's little street, consisting of just 30 houses, there were three other families that had adopted children. Unfortunately life for a single parent wasn't made easy back then and they did not get the support that is available to them today. Single parents were made to feel ashamed and adoption was hidden. Back then, if a child that was to be given up for adoption was baptised before they were adopted; only a pencil entry would be made in the register book. Then, when the child was formally adopted, the entry would be altered, inserting the adoptive parents' names as though they had been present. Even to this day the law regarding adoption is outdated and in need of change.

In the days after leaving the hospital there was no time to waste and Mum and dad began writing their first letter to the adoption agency – a follow up to the initial enquiries they had already made to start the process.

To whom it may concern,

We wish to apply to your adoption agency with regards to the prospect of adopting a child. Father Brown in our local parish has suggested to us that we contact your agency for information.

We would be very grateful if you could assist us by providing the necessary information and an application form.

Kind regards,

M and M

Not much time passed when they received their first response from the adoption agency, which read...

Dear M and M,

Thank you very much for your letter. I received your letter
informing us of your wish to adopt. I have the pleasure in
sending you the initial application forms and we will leave
a copy of the application form for you also at our reception,
as I understand the postal strike is ongoing. Perhaps I could
ask you both to call in to see me on Wednesday next at 4pm
when we could discuss the factors involved. You can bring the
completed forms with you. I hope this appointment will be
convenient.
I look forward to meeting you.

Sincerely,
Sarah (Adoption worker)

My parents would soon realise that the regulations were extremely strict and
they came across their first hurdle when they received the application forms.
    One of these indepth forms read as follows:

Application form

The information given by applicants on this form will
be treated in strict confidence
Name and address ....
Phone number...
Date of birth of husband ....
Date of birth of wife ....
What is your income? ....
State nature and place of employment...
Particulars of life insurance..
Are you both in good health? ....
Date and place of marriage ....
Have you any children?...
(If so state name and age) ....
Has any child been adopted by you before? ....
Give particulars ....
Have you ever applied to any other adoption agency?

....
What is the accommodation of your home? ....

Do you both wish to adopt a child?..
Have you fully considered the matter? ....
Why do you wish to adopt a child? ....
Have you any preference regarding sex and age of the child?
....
Are you BOTH practicing Catholics?..
Give name and address of a responsible person
(not a relative) who can vouch for you......................................
....
....
Signature of husband ....
Signature of wife..
Date ....

Note - Following the initial interview, the parish priest, employer's references and medical certificates will be required. The society does not give its reason for refusing to accept an application.

Applications from couples wishing to adopt can only be considered if both applicants are over the age of 25 at least 3 years married and under the age of 45 (husband) and 40 years (wife).

Initially they were filling out the application without many problems until it came to the very last sentence on the page. They hadn't yet been married three years and if they were to wait until they had been married a full three years mum would already be 40.

Did this mean an end to adopting a child before they had even fully started the process? It was back to the drawing board and they wrote to the agency once more to clarify the issue, explaining their own circumstances and hoping there was a way around it.

Again they waited. Waited for the phone to ring. Waited for the post to come.

Chapter 2 – "One way or another, we will have children"

September 21st 1979

Dear Mr and Mrs M,

Further to our recent correspondence I have now put your particular circumstances before our committee for consideration. They have agreed that in the event of you still being interested in adoption by late spring 1980, they will then be prepared to consider your application.
I will be pleased therefore, if one way or another, you would perhaps let me know your circumstances by about April of next year.

With kind wishes,
Yours sincerely,
Sarah (Adoption worker)

IT wasn't exactly the news that they were hoping for. They had already been trying for a baby for so long, but all the same they were so grateful that the door hadn't been closed on them and there was still a chance for them to adopt a baby that they had both wanted so much.

In the months that followed, they tried as much as possible to get on with their lives, going to work, having nights out like any other couple that had no children. It was always in the back of their minds though, waiting for April to come so that they could proceed with their application.

Just as soon as the time arrived, they wrote to the adoption agency and informed them that nothing had changed on their part and they were still as eager as ever to continue and hopefully be approved to adopt a child.

April 1st 1980

Dear Mr and Mrs M,

Thank you for your letter informing me that you would like to proceed with your adoption application.
I would therefore like to arrange to meet both of you again and I wonder could I ask you to call here to see me on Wednesday April 16th at 4pm. I hope this appointment will be convenient and I look forward to meeting you both again.

Yours sincerely,
Sarah (Adoption worker)

The day eventually arrived and, full of anticipation, mum and dad went to meet the adoption worker. Walking into the office and meeting a lady who was going to decide whether or not she believed they were suited to being a parent was a nerve-racking experience for them. They had already lost the ability to make that decision for themselves.

A decision made and often at times taken for granted by so many. Now their future as parents lay in the hands of this social worker. A stranger! It seemed so unfair, but they were determined to do whatever was necessary.

The familiar feeling of the air being sucked right out of the room was there when my dad reached for the big brass handle to knock on the door. Once he heard the footsteps of somebody walking through the hallway, he stepped back and reached out to take mum's hand. They were greeted by a smiling middle-aged lady who was neatly dressed in a long skirt and blouse.

"You must be Mr and Mrs McNamara? I am delighted to finally have the opportunity to meet with you both, I am Sarah."

They were directed into the slim dark hallway and up the stairs, all the time mum trying to silence the voices in her head.

What if she doesn't like us? I can't even remember the questions we had prepared to ask, I should have written them down. Why would she give us a child over another couple? This has to go well; please God let it go well.

Before she knew it they were sitting down and had been offered a cup of tea, which they both refused.

"I am sure you are both eager to get started."

Mum and dad both looked at each other with a nervous grin while Sarah took out their file with a pen in hand.

"OK, so you have decided adoption is something you would like to consider, tell me a little bit about yourself and how you came to the conclusion that adoption is for you."

Mum let dad take the lead while she tried to convince herself to relax.

"Are you fully aware of how difficult a process this can be?" asked Sarah.

Mum knew she had the answer to that question, as for them there was nothing as difficult as being told that they could not have children in their lives. She smiled at Sarah, finding her confidence.

"We are prepared to go through anything to have a family. I believe we would make good parents, in fact I know we would. I understand it will not be an easy process but what in life, that is worth having, is easy?"

They were beginning to realise, as they answered each ones of Sarah's questions, that all she needed them to be was themselves and by the time some of the more difficult questions came up they were on a roll – every question taking them another step closer to having the family they always dreamed about. Between them they explained to Sarah in as much detail as she needed about their emotional, financial, physical and spiritual state of mind and before they knew it nearly two hours had passed. Sarah finally placed her pen down on the table.

"I realise that this is not easy for anyone so thank you for being so open and honest with me. The next step will be a home visit so we can assess the environment that you would be bringing a child into. It is nothing to worry about and you are doing great."

She led them back down the stairs and into the dark hallway where they finally found themselves back on the doorstep.

"We will write to you in due course. It was lovely to meet you both."

And with that the door closed behind them.

"Mac I feel weak and emotionally drained, I don't know what I will do if we have put ourselves through all of this for nothing."

Dad, understanding exactly how she felt, didn't need to say a word and they began to walk arm in arm through the city centre in silence. Eventually he found the strength to say, "The only thing we would ever regret, love, is if we didn't try. Let's show them what we are made of and really go for it."

Drained, but excited, scared, but hopeful, in that moment my parents reminded themselves, that even though that first meeting had felt like a police interview and it took a lot out of them, they now had to put their money where their mouths were and do whatever it took to have a family of their very own.

And with that mum turned to dad with a loving smile and repeated the words to him that he had said to her in her weakest moments, "One way or another, we will have children."

*

Anyone who has ever had the experience of adopting a child will know how difficult and draining the process is. Yes, it is very exciting, but you have to be prepared for it and the fact that at any time your child could be taken away from you. Like a marathon, you don't know if you will get to the finish line. When my mum would tell me how hard and intrusive the process was, she would still always finish by saying, "That is what they had to do, so I don't mind. The child has to be the centre of it all and they had to be sure they were placing him/her in a happy, secure and stable environment."

I believe that keeping that in her mind helped her to get through the process more easily.

After that initial meeting they continued eagerly through the process. Garda checks, financial checks, reference checks and home visits. Mum gave up her job because they preferred one parent to be at home full-time with the child and she wanted to show her commitment to it any way she could.

After all the checks were completed and home visit after home visit was done, the waiting game began, again. Waiting for the phone to ring, waiting for the post to come, waiting to become the parents they knew they were always meant to be.

And finally the day came! A day, which started out like any other – until the postman dropped that letter through the door.

Dear Mr and Mrs M,

This is a letter to confirm that your case went in front of the board and your application to adopt your first baby has been approved by our committee. Your name is now officially on our waiting list. I hope we will be contacting you shortly.

Warmest regards,
Sarah (Adoption worker)

That one letter would change their lives forever. It was their pregnancy test – the only difference being that they had no idea how long they were going to be pregnant for!

Waiting! Waiting for the post to come, waiting for the phone to ring! This became a constant in the weeks that followed, but it was just something they had to deal with. This time though, it was for the news that a child had been chosen for them and so waiting for that was a little bit easier. They had been asked at the very beginning, if it was a girl or a boy that they would prefer? Mum's answer was, if they were having a baby the "normal" way, they would not get to make that decision and so she didn't want to make it now. They wanted to leave it in the hands of God.

Then one day the phone rang. Mum, her arms full of washing, was on her way up the stairs as she walked past it.

Distracted and trying not to drop all of the clothes she eventually managed to pick up the receiver and balance it between her cheek and shoulder.

"Hello?"

"Hi, Mrs Mc Namara, this is Sarah here from the adoption agency."

Within seconds the clothes dropped to the floor.

"Hello, Sarah, how nice to hear from you," mum replied, in her best telephone voice before closing her eyes and silently praying for good news.

"I will get straight to why I have phoned. I am absolutely delighted to tell you that the board have met and we have matched you up with a baby. You are going to have a son."

With that mum let out the scream she had been holding inside since that day back in the hospital when they were told they could not have children.

Dad had been in the garden, where he was busy planting a new tree, but raced into the house when he heard mum's scream, afraid that there may be something wrong. He was greeted, however, by the sight of his wife in the middle of the hallway, sitting on the floor on top of a pile of washing, still on the phone with tears streaming down her face.

The biggest smile, he had ever seen on her face, however, was unmistakeable.

"Are you ok?" Realising the shock mum was in, Sarah pressed her down the line.

"Sarah, I can't tell you, I can't find the words to say how grateful we are. Thank you doesn't seem appropriate."

She could almost hear Sarah smile. "Let me tell you a little bit about your son. He is a beautiful little 10-week-old boy, with a big mop of golden brown hair and the most beautiful smile – the kind that lights up a room. I can't wait for you to meet him and take him home. How would Tuesday suit? I could have him here by lunchtime?"

With my dad still full of muck from the garden, and them both now sitting in the hall on top of a pile of clean washing, he watched mum's face intently, but in silence. It took just a couple more minutes for her to take the rest of the details from Sarah and eventually hang up the phone, after which she turned to face my dad.

Looking at him with tears flowing down his face she hugged him tight and whispered gently in his ear, "We have a son my love, we are finally going to have our family. We have a son!"

*

The day their lives would change forever finally came and they left with an empty carrycot and walked with it in the centre of town towards the

12

adoption agency. I can't imagine what must have been going through their minds that day, looking at that empty carrycot but knowing that they would be bringing home a baby in it, just a few short hours later.

When they reached the agency, and knocked on the big green door, they took a step back and waited for it to be opened on their new life. The adoption worker, who knew them quite well at this stage, led them up three flights of stairs to the top of the building, and brought them into a big spacious room with large windows overlooking the city.

It was here that they met their son and as he was put into my mother's arms the tears they shed were, finally, ones of utter joy.

The day you meet your child for the first time, no matter what way it happens, whether it be in the delivery room of a hospital or a few weeks later in an adoption agency, it is unlike any other feeling in the world. Only a mother could understand that level of love and happiness. A feeling so strong you didn't even know it was possible until that very day. It is amazing, but for my parents the official side of things also kept them grounded for a short while and the next thing they knew they were signing a form, which all too harshly reminded them that it was by no means the end of the story. This baby, their son, could (for whatever reason) still be taken away from them at any point over the next 12 months. It would be a full year before the final adoption papers would be signed and at any stage during that year, the birth mother was within her rights to change her mind and take her baby back.

The form clarified this:

We the undersigned agree to care for Carl, born on the 22nd of May 1980, who has been placed with us with the view of adoption.

We recognise that the child's placement is on a probationary basis until the society is satisfied and ready to allow us to proceed with an application for an adoption order under the adoption act. Should the society wish to remove the child from our care, for any reason whatsoever, prior to our legal adoption of the child, we agree to hand the child back to the care of the society.

We agree to remain resident in the Republic of Ireland until we have the child adopted legally or return him to the society.

We undertake to bring the child up in the knowledge that he is adopted.

Signed (husband) ....

Signed (wife) ....

I understand that a contract was necessary for the protection of any child in this situation, but it seemed so cold. My parents, however, were just so happy that they had been given the chance to become parents and nothing could break their elation. They hadn't even left the room before they fell in love with him.

The adoption worker carried Carl down the stairs, as mum wasn't allowed to carry him until they were outside the building, in case she fell. Finally, over the big green doorway, with the adoption worker on one side and my mum on the other, she handed him over. Their first child was now coming home.

On the way home my dad did what every new father would do. He drove the car more carefully than ever before and after a quick stopover at my mum's family home to introduce their new son to the family, they brought Carl home and placed him in his new cot.

Like every new parent they were thrown straight in at the deep end with nappies, bottles and night feeds. The only significant difference being that they were bonding with a new little bundle that they were almost afraid to call their own. They tried to put the thought to the back of their minds but there was no denying that at any stage he could be taken away from them. So every time the phone would ring, they got a fearful chill. It didn't help matters when someone they had known had adopted a child a few months before them experienced worst case scenario. The birth mother changed her mind and took the child back. They knew that they could not live their lives in fear though and so they just decided to enjoy every moment with Carl. At the end of the day, they realised, adoption or not, nobody knows what tomorrow will bring and the only thing any of us have is right now.

And so they went through all the "firsts," that every parent does with a new baby. The first smile, the first laugh, the first time they get sick, the first time they sleep through the night, the first time they crawl and the first, unsure, steps they take towards getting on their feet. With every day that passed my parents were falling deeper and deeper in love, until finally that year had passed and, yet again, they found themselves waiting.
Waiting for the phone to ring, waiting for the post to come!

By then Carl was very much their son, their little boy, and all they wanted was for it to be made official.

May 26th 1981

With reference to your application for an adoption order, I have been directed by the board to say that your case has been listed for hearing at 4pm on Thursday the 4th of June 1981. It will be necessary for both of you to attend with the child. If it is not possible for the child to be present due to illness, a medical certificate to that effect should be furnished at the hearing.

You should notify the board immediately if this notice is insufficient or if, for some other reason, you are unable to attend the above date. In that event, alternative arrangements will be made for the hearing of your case.

4th June 1981

With reference to your application for an adoption order in respect of the child, Carl, I am directed by the board to inform you that at a meeting held on the 4th of June 1981, the board made an order granting your application.

It is now open to you to apply for an amended birth certificate in respect of the child. The short form birth certificate costs 25p if the application is made in person and 30p if the application is made by post. The long form of the amended birth certificate costs 47p if the application is made in person and 52p if the application is made by post. I am to state that the long form of a birth certificate is required for children allowance purposes, under the social welfare act.

I enclose a copy of this letter, which should be forwarded when you are applying for a birth certificate.

So there it was! The day they had been waiting for, for so long. They could breathe again. Not only did they have their son with them, but he was legally their son now too. No more waiting for the phone to ring, waiting for the post to come. It was one of the happiest days of their lives and finally they could get on with living it…

Chapter 3 – "You're not finished with us yet!"

I'M thinking that maybe they missed seeing the postman!

It wasn't too long after that day that the social worker came out to the house for an "after visit." She wanted to see how they were getting on and congratulated them on everything becoming legal. It was on that day that my mum took the opportunity to tell her, "You're not finished with us yet! You know we will be applying for number two!"

They remembered the agency telling them that the last thing that they wanted to see is an only child and that they would (if possible), want them to go on to have brothers and sisters. So my parents didn't even give themselves space to breathe before they started the process all over again. I don't know where they got their strength, but I am so glad that they did!

This time was slightly different in that they were also managing a little boy who had just found his feet, as well as all the application forms, interviews, checks and home visits. They did, however, find the process a little bit easier, being familiar with the system and knowing what to expect. It was back to the ups and downs, back to the waiting and excitement, but my parents wanted a second baby just as badly as the first and they were happy and prepared to jump through any hoops that were put in front of them. Inevitably, though, in the back of their minds, they hadn't forgotten about the last line of the adoption application form;

Applications from couples wishing to adopt can only be considered if both applicants are over the age of 25, at least three years married and under the age of 45(husband) and 40 (wife).

When they were adopting Carl, their hurdle was that they were not yet three years married but this time my mum was over the age of 40. There were so many other couples out there that wanted children just as much as they did, and ticked every last box on the application forms, that they were scared they would be overlooked.

They weren't going to let anything stop them from trying though. I asked my dad in the years since why they persisted with the application form when they already knew that they were technically no longer eligible because of their age and he told me that it was a requirement put in place by the adoption agency. It was not law and that they knew they would be able to show anyone at the agency that they would make good parents. They were already good parents to Carl and it would also be nice for him to have a sister or brother so they hoped the adoption board would use its discretion and let them proceed with their second application.

As it turned out they were right. The board knew mum and dad already and the members had seen how they had handled the long difficult process of adopting Carl. They also saw a little boy, happy and settled with his new parents, so when it came to filling out another application form they didn't hesitate.

It wasn't long this time before the postman came again, delivering the letter that told them that they were now, again, officially on the waiting list to adopt a child. They could not have imagined that less than two years after that day in Holles Street, in the doctor's office where they were told that they would not have children, they would be the proud parents of a one-year-old little boy while waiting for a second child.

It just shows how much anyone's life can change, in a very short space of time, if you push for your goals.

Their goal was a family and they both had to work so hard to get it. It's something that happens so easily for so many people and I would never have blamed them if they had felt cheated. All they had to do was open their front door to see friends, family and neighbours all having babies. But they simply kept focused on their goals and, as they say, "left it in the hands of God." My parents live their lives with a very strong faith in God and this was, and would often prove to be over the years, their saving grace.

Chapter 4 – Gaining a daughter

ON the same side of the city, while mum and dad were still waiting, I was born on the 10th of February 1982. My birth mother, Mary, was twenty four years old, alone and scared. In her final year of college she felt that she could not confide in any of her family throughout her pregnancy and simply didn't want to let her parents, who had been so proud of her, down. Irish society in those days did not make it easy for single parents. Young girls out of wedlock were made to feel ashamed and were sent away, hidden from friends, family, relatives and neighbours, to have their babies. It was so wrong that the support wasn't there for them. It was a different Ireland. Mary's family believed she had been taken to the hospital for a different reason. They had no idea that she was about to deliver a baby and so she went through labour alone and scared, just like she had been the whole nine months. During those painful contractions she tried to stay strong remembering the chats she had with me in her bedroom on those dark lonely nights at home before I was born. She would sit in her room releasing all the pain and tension caused by spending her day trying to conceal her growing belly. She didn't have to hide in her bedroom, she could be herself, she could cry and she could talk and sing to me – so that is what she did.

"You are my sunshine,
my only sunshine.
You make me happy, when skies are grey.
Don't you know dear, how much I love you?
Please don't take my sunshine away."

She would look at her growing belly with so much love but so much fear at the same time and she made a promise every night.

"I will figure this out for you. You are the only person I can talk to right now. Don't feel alone, don't feel scared. I love you."

Mary gave birth to me in the delivery suite in Holles Street, surrounded by strangers. After all, the midwives and doctors there were the only other people, in the world, who knew her secret. So she prayed that they would see her pain and support her because even through the fear, she had been looking forward to having our chats, the ones that had become part of her daily routine, but with me in her arms. And maybe, just maybe, she thought, that would be what would give her the strength and support she needed to face her family, to face the world as a single parent.

As fate would have it though, she would never be given that chance. After the delivery, the hospital learned that she had not informed anyone of her pregnancy so they moved her away from me, and the postnatal ward, so that nobody would ask questions. Mary was discharged from the hospital the following day after being given an appointment card for an adoption agency and sent on her way. No support or counselling was offered. I stayed in the hospital for a week or so and the nurses there looked after me, while decisions were made as to where I would be placed.

During her pregnancy Mary had been so frightened that anyone would find out, that she had spent her time trying to act normal. She would try to put it to the back of her mind during the day, so she could pretend it wasn't happening, until we had our time together alone in her bedroom at night. She didn't want to let her parents down but she felt so drained and so constantly tired that when it eventually came to the day I was born, she still hadn't fully decided what she was going to do. So, afterwards, she walked through the city centre and found herself at the big green door of the adoption agency – where she had been told to go by the hospital staff. She reached out and shyly knocked on the door but remained standing in the shadows instead of standing back into the street. Eventually a middle-aged lady pulled open the heavy door and, with a smile, greeted her.

"Hi, my name is Mary and I was told by the midwives, after I had my baby, to come and speak to you here."

"Of course dear, come on in you look freezing. My name is Sarah. Take a seat and I will put the kettle on."

Mary sat in the middle of an empty room not fully knowing why she was there or what to say, so she began the only way she knew how, by uttering the words out loud for the first time.

"I have just had a baby. I have told nobody and I really need some help."

Hearing the words outside of her head for the first time, and away from the comforts of her bedroom, led Mary to break down in tears.

"I don't know what the right thing to do is and I am scared," she managed between sobs.

Sarah looked at her with pity as she recognised the pain in her eyes and stood up from her chair, moving it so as to sit by Mary, and held her hand.

"It is OK dear. You have done the right thing coming here and don't be afraid, we can help. Have you considered adoption?"

"I couldn't allow myself to think about it, but now my baby is here and she is alone in the hospital. It is such a mess," whispered Mary.

"My dear, we can deal with this together."

Mary listened intently as Sarah explained her options and talked her through the process involved in putting a child up for adoption. She sat there listening and her heart slowly began to break in two as she came to the realisation that adoption may be what was best for me. She tried to take comfort from Sarah telling her that it takes strength for anyone to make that decision and that both she and Mary knew she would be doing it out of love.

Mary left that day feeling more comfortable, having had the strength to say out loud the words she had been screaming inside her head for so long. She also left that day feeling more alone than ever. Eventually though, she decided, for only reasons she knows, that adoption was the best way forward for me and I have to say that I am so grateful that she was brave enough to make that decision for me.

After that, arrangements were made for me to leave the hospital and I went to stay in a foster home with a lady I know only as Mrs O'Brien. Mrs O'Brien would regularly stay in touch with the adoption agency and supply up-to-date information regarding my progress.

Some of the information recorded was as follows:

3rd March 1982

The baby is a very pretty little baby with dark hair and complexion. She sleeps and feeds well and there are absolutely no problems, according to Mrs O'Brien. Mrs O'Brien has no details on the baby i.e. whether she has had her B.C.G or P.K.U. If she has not had these done then Mrs O'Brien will arrange them immediately. We are to let her know.

1st April 1982

Baby is coming along very well. She was back last Thursday for her six-week check. She now weighs 9 lbs. 4ozs and Holles Street were very pleased with her. She had both her B.C.G and P.K.U last week. She came out in a rash after the B.C.G but this has now totally cleared up. She is a pretty-looking baby, petite and has small features, a pale complexion and auburn coloured hair. She eats and sleeps well. She is not baptised.

By the time I was 10 weeks old it was time for me to leave my foster home for my permanent home. My parents were overjoyed. The time had finally come to complete their long-awaited family. The letter that started my journey to my new family stated that their new baby daughter had arrived. Life suddenly switched into high gear again. After all the waiting they suddenly had less than a week to organise everything before they were to come and collect me. Again they walked through Dublin city centre with their empty carrycot in one hand, but this time holding the little hand of my brother in the other.

How life had changed.

Again they knocked on the big heavy green door, again they walked up all of the flight of stairs to the top of the building and again they entered the big room with the windows overlooking the city. The same room in which they had first met their son.

Finally their family was complete.

Their determination had paid off. Two children they could call their own. Life couldn't get much better.

My brother, however, was not too impressed with all of the fuss over the new little person. By that stage he was nearly two years old and was used to having our parents all to himself. The day my mum took me out of the car for the first time, at our home, my dad had the camcorder out and captured the moment Carl blocked the doorway saying; "This is my house". They had to convince him to let me in the front door. He forgave me eventually and he accepted our family of four!

*

As life has a habit of doing, and just as it seemed things couldn't get any better, it threw them a curve ball. We had all just arrived home that day and Mum had settled me off to sleep in her arms when the phone rang and woke me. Passing her crying daughter to my dad she then casually walked to answer it.

"Hello?"

It was her sister.

"Is Mac there with you?"

"Yes, of course, we have just arrived back from a walk with the kids. It was so funny you should have seen Carl trying to push Aoife in her pram and he....."

"M, wait a second"

"I have some bad news, it is dad…he has passed away."

21

Devastated, Mum found herself sitting on the same spot in the hallway where she and dad had sat when they first found out that they were going to become parents. Again my dad came to sit with her and again, in that same spot on the floor, they cried together – but this time he had one arm around her and one cradling his new baby daughter.

So as well as being a very happy year, that one was also a very sad and difficult time for our family. But my mum is the most amazing and strong lady I've ever known; and she held her head high, and together with her family, dealt with her loss.

Chapter 5 – Knock Knock

ONCE again in the months that followed, mum and dad had to try and put to the back of their minds the fact that at any stage my birth mother could change her mind and that I could be taken off them, until the final papers were signed, which would not be for nearly a year. They tried to trust that everything was going to be OK and they had already been through this with Carl, so they settled into life again with all of the night feeds, nappies, bottles and loads of play time that we required. Of course, now and then, that helpless feeling crept in on them, causing gut-wrenching fear as they also fell deeper and deeper in love with their little girl. But, as before, they decided that they would do whatever it took to protect their new little family – they couldn't help that this was the one thing that was totally out of their control.

One evening when my dad came home from work he found mum sitting in the back garden on the grass with me in her arms while she watched Carl chase the next-door neighbours' cat, Fluffy, around the sand pit.

"Hi, love, I'm home," he shouted from the kitchen window.

Mum didn't come inside to greet him as she normally would so he popped the kettle on and walked outside.

"Daddy," Carl yelled as he raced up the garden path to greet him.

After giving his son a welcoming hug he sat down on the grass next to mum and gently kissed my forehead as I quietly slept.

"Everything ok love? Smile it might not happen," he joked when he noticed the sad look on her face.

"Mac look at her, so peaceful, I would die if she wanted her back. I never knew we could love anything the way we love Carl and Aoife, I can't bear it every time the phone rings."

"I know M, but you can't think of things like that. Aoife has been our daughter from the moment we laid eyes on her and you just need to have a little faith. There is no reason that will ever change, just you wait and see, but until it is all official we just have to push it to the back of our minds and enjoy every second of our perfect little family. Nobody knows what tomorrow will bring."

She smiled, in agreement, at my dad and carefully placed me in his arms.

"Come on, Carl, let's get you washed up for dinner," she said as she took hold of his little hand and wandered back up the garden path and into the house.

It was times like that, when they helped each other through the hard moments, that helped the year pass and before they knew it they found themselves, one last time, waiting for the postman to come – and he did.

On a day like any other, Mum heard him coming and made her way into the hall. Flicking through the bills she immediately noticed a letter, different from the others, and she knew in her heart it was from the adoption agency. With baited breath she teased open the envelope and as fast as her eyes could follow she scanned the pages, not having the patience to read it from the start, until she came to that all important sentence.

I am desired by the board to inform you that an adoption order has been granted to you in respect of the child, Aoife. It is now open to you to apply for an amended birth certificate in respect of this child.

Clutching the letter tightly in her hand and with her tears falling on the pages she raced to the phone to call my dad.

"Mac, it's me, she is ours! Our baby daughter is finally all ours."

*

During those first few years, the adoption agency would keep in touch from time to time to see how things were going and the conversation always seemed to come around to the same topic. They would tell my mum that Carl's birth mother was regularly in touch and that she was struggling, although she knew that adoption was the right thing for him. She was very keen to know how he was getting on and that he was happy. They asked if mum would be willing to write Carl's birth mother a letter to tell her how he was doing, but not to feel under any pressure if she wasn't comfortable. Mum, being the amazing lady that she is, said "absolutely no problem at all." As she sat at the kitchen table with a pen and paper, attempting to write Carl's birth mother a letter, she stopped for a moment and leaned her chair back to look into the living room where Carl and I were playing with Lego. She watched quietly, with a private smile at us getting on so well together, and thought to herself… *Not family from blood but family in every other way, what a perfect little family we have. How will I find the words to comfort the woman who, in order to give me my dreams, had to give up her own. It has been six years since she last seen the son she gave to us, and what a gift he has been.*

All of a sudden, while watching us play, it became clear what she hoped Carl's birth mother would take comfort from and she wrote a letter telling her about all the major milestones in his life. His funny little personality and how well he got on with his little sister. She felt the sadness in her heart as she wrote, realising that the reason for all the happiness in her life was the same reason for someone else's pain.

Each time mum had contact from the adoption agency she would ask the same question;
"Is there any word from Aoife's birth mother?"
Each time the adoption lady would shake her head and say, "Not a word."

This was something which was painfully ironic in the years to come, because it was me, as it turned out, that was more affected by the fact I was adopted and was constantly looking for any little bit of information. Carl, on the other hand, was just happy to get on with the life he had been given with my parents.

We had no idea, however, that Mary was going through struggles of her own. She had been trying to deal with the hole left in her life after I was gone and was struggling with the questions that haunted her.

Where is my baby?

Is she OK?

I pray to God I have done the right thing for her.

At the same time, mum was dealing with the sudden death of her own father, but as kids we knew nothing of this – all we knew was silence.

Chapter 6 – "It's not good news"

"MRS McNamara, there is no other way this say this…you have Cancer. The tests have been concluded on the biopsy and all I can say at this time is that we have a complicated situation here and I am sorry it is not good news."

"Cancer? I couldn't have. I am too young, I feel fine. Cancer! Really?"

"I am afraid anybody can get Cancer at any time and you have just been unlucky. We will need to proceed with a full mastectomy, which has been scheduled in for Thursday."

Losing all of the power in her body her thoughts turned to her husband and her children and in desperation my mum cried out, "I can't die, not now."

To which the doctor simply replied, "we will do everything we can," before turning to walk away, leaving mum alone with the nurse who was still standing at the end of her bed in silence.

"Please nurse, I need to phone my husband. Could you show me where the payphone is?"

But dismissing her request the nurse replied, "Now what would you want to do that for? Wasn't that your husband who was here with you this morning? Leave him be for the afternoon, nothing will change between now and this evening's visiting hours. Stay in bed and have a rest after that shock."

With no compassion whatsoever she then turned and left my mum alone.

Alone with the word CANCER. Alone with her tears. Alone with her fears. Fears for herself, fears for her family, her husband and her children. She had fought so hard for the life she had, a life she couldn't help but think might now be taken away from her.

It seemed like an eternity before my dad walked back on to the ward and as soon as she saw his smiling face pop out from behind a huge bouquet of flowers, any strength she had been trying to portray left her.

"Hi, love, the kids chose these flowers for you. Aoife made me pick the ones with the sunflowers because she said their faces always look like they are smiling."

"Mac, I have Cancer."

She couldn't bear to see the look of pain and disbelief on my dad's face so she turned and buried her head in the pillow, trying to control her tears.

It was as if behind this hospital curtain their whole world had been ripped apart but in a simple show of love and support my dad simply lay down beside his wife and held her. No questions needed to be asked right then. For now they would cry and grieve together.

"You will get through this, love. You are stronger than anyone else I know. Never stop thinking about our beautiful children. They will get you through this and I will be right here by your side."

I had turned five that week, and despite everything going on mum, somehow, found the strength to make sure she pulled out all of the stops for me. To me everything was normal, I was just so excited about my birthday, but to this day I don't know where she found the strength from, to wear a smiling mask.

*

Mum was taken into hospital on the Thursday, after spending the morning with us. Carl and I didn't know why we had the day off school but we were preoccupied and excited because my mum's friend Doreen was coming to pick us up and bring us to the park and McDonald's.

I sat on mum's bed watching her pack her bag.

"Mummy, where are you going?" I asked.

"I have to go back into the hospital for a little while, darling, so the doctor can make me better."

"But Mummy you don't look sick and I will miss you at night. Daddy can't make the hot chocolate like you do. His one always has lumps."

Mum managed a smile and made a promise, "How about I take a break from this and we can all go and have some hot chocolate now? I can show daddy how to make it just right. I won't be able to have any, but that just means more for you and Carl."

"Carl," I shouted down the stairs. "Mum's going to make hot chocolate!"

Carl and I sat looking out of the window that day missing our mum before she even left, watching our dad help her into the car and drive away. Our tears stopped soon after though with Doreen's voice coming from the kitchen.

"Right you two, who wants to go to the park?"

"I do, I do," we shouted.

Doreen moved into the house while mum was in hospital so my dad could be free and my mum wouldn't be by herself so much.

She was such a special person in my life and even though she sadly passed away when I was eight, I have always felt that she has been with me throughout my life – like a guardian angel. She was there for mum too when she needed her most.

Mum had a full mastectomy and her first round of chemotherapy while she was still in hospital. She was so sick and in so much pain, but she always put on a smile for us when we were brought in to see her. I raced through the long hospital corridors and jumped up on her tall bed, every time, just to remind myself of that very smile. One of the things I remember from that time was how much I missed my mum. A five-year-old girl needed her mummy and I couldn't wait until she came home to us. It was impossible to understand, at that age, why things weren't the same at home without her. I just knew I needed her home. We all did.

When the day finally arrived for her to leave hospital she was still fairly weak from the surgery and the chemo, but nothing was going to stop her from smiling that day. My dad arrived to take her home and she was already packed, dressed and impatiently waiting at the side of her bed when he turned into the ward with a wheelchair to take her to the car.

"Beep, beep," he joked. "Your carriage awaits, my love."

Mum quickly by-passed the wheelchair though and told him, "There is life left in me yet. There were times when I didn't think I would be leaving this hospital but now that I am I won't be leaving in a wheelchair. Let's go home."

Dad took her bag in one hand and linked her arm with the other.

"There is nowhere else I would rather take you, my love. I haven't told the kids, it is a surprise."

Carl and I had been playing in the garden when dad's car pulled up. I was getting annoyed at my brother because he kept trying to beat up my teddies with wrestling moves, while I was trying to play teddy bears' picnic. Our fighting was interrupted, however, by dad beeping his horn and we immediately noticed mum's smiling face sitting in the passenger seat so we raced to greet her. As soon as we could open the door we jumped on to her lap.

"Slow down kids, be careful of your mum. She is still a little sore from the hospital," dad cried out.

So Carl took her bag and I took her hand and we all went inside, closing the door behind us.

"What's for dinner Mum? Can you make me hot chocolate? Dad still can't make it as good as you can."

She smiled at me as she slowly, lowered herself into her favourite armchair and replied, "It's good to be home."

The relief for her, at being home, was obvious but she looked so tired. It is one of my earliest memories and one I will never forget, but I was just so happy that mummy was home. I assumed as she was home she was better, but she still had such a long, hard road to travel with chemo sessions right for much of the rest of the year. She won't agree with me even now, but my mum is one of the strongest people I know and I am now, and always have been, so proud of her. So proud she is my mum.

*

During that year my gran (mum's mum) was turning eighty and mum has told me in the years since, that she didn't think she was going to be alive to see her mother reach that milestone. They were planning a surprise party for her, which I ruined by racing up the driveway to my gran's house one day and blurting out, "I know something you don't know and it's about your birthday party."

Everyone got a good laugh out of it, which is just what they needed.

Mum was living that year as if it was her last, enjoying time with my dad, my brother and I. She thought time was going to be taken away from her, so she was refusing to waste any of it. We even went on our first family holiday that year to Spain, even though she was feeling incredibly sick.

It turned out not to be mum's last year though, thank God. She fought hard and finally beat Cancer! Eventually she could get past thinking about this horrible disease that threatened to take her life and she started to live and enjoy life again.

To this day though, she refuses to make any long-term plans. Whenever I ask her about something in the future, (like a holiday) I always still get the same reply, "I don't know if I'll be here tomorrow let alone next year."

It was a life lesson that has never left her.

Chapter 7 – Adoption and me

EVER since I understood what the word adoption meant, it was always a huge part of my life. I felt a lack of identity and finding out my birth mother's story was something I always needed to do. I wanted to understand what she went through. It was never a maybe or a question for me. I always knew that as soon as I turned eighteen, I would try and search for her.

Maybe it is because I had such a great childhood, but I never really thought much past meeting her and hearing her story, knowing my history, where I came from and why? I never imagined that we could have a relationship past that. Maybe I thought that because she gave me up, she wouldn't want to have that relationship. It turned out to be one of the most important lessons that I have ever learned – Never assume you know how other people are feeling and know that all people are capable of change. In a good way and in a bad way!

As the years went on the fact that I was adopted became more and more a part of my life. It became more complicated in my head and I felt such a range of emotions about it. How can something make you happy and sad at the same time? Rejected and loved, all at once? For a teenager, all these feelings were very confusing.

Although I had a very happy childhood, happy and secure within a close family, going on holidays, having birthday parties and day trips, this feeling never fully went away. And although I was never sensitive about being adopted and was able to speak about it to my friends and family freely, it still felt like there was something missing in my life, even when I was as young as 10 or 11. And so I found myself thinking more and more about being adopted.

There was a piece of paper given to my parents, when I was adopted, and it read:

> Aoife's birth mother was age 24 years at the time of her birth. She is the eldest in her family and is a twin. Her name is Mary and she is from Dublin. She is a lovely looking girl, about 5'3" height with green eyes and fair hair. She has a bright lively personality. She passed her leaving certificate and is a nurse. Her hobbies include art and music and she plays the guitar. Aoife's birth father was age 26 years. He is from the country and works on the family farm. He is 5'10 in height with brown hair and brown eyes. He had a full secondary education. His interests are football, hurling and music. He plays the guitar and mandolin. The birth mother did not confide in her parents or any of her family about the pregnancy. She confided in the birth father but he was not very supportive and there was no question of marriage. Mary decided on adoption for Aoife as she felt it offered her the security and stability of a two-parent family, which she herself could not provide.

When I started to talk to my mum more, and ask more questions, she gave this piece of paper to me, thinking it might help. I found myself reading it over and over thinking, *Is this it? Is this all I am ever going to know about my history? Did this lady, Mary, ever care about me? Why did she leave? Was it my fault? Did she ever think about me? Have I ever walked by her in the street? Did she miss me in her life?*

These questions (and there were so many) caused me so much pain as a teenager. It was all so confusing. Adoption made me feel loved and safe as a little girl, so I couldn't understand why, all of a sudden, the same thing was causing all these other feelings?

The older I got, however, the more I realised that all these feelings (good and bad) were normal when on the adoption path. Every story has its good parts and bad – mine was no different.

*

I was thirteen years old when I realised it would be years before I would be able to search for some answers. This wait built it up in my head and I don't think I was able for it, or knew how to handle it.

One night as a programme about Irish adoptions came on the telly I got really upset. Perhaps other times the programme wouldn't have got a reaction from me at all but that day it really mattered – that day it hurt… because that day was my birthday.

I remember quietly leaving the room and going up to lie on my bed. Adoption had already ruined so many of my birthdays. *Why did I have to watch that today?* I wondered. But it was too late, once I saw it I couldn't switch it off. I wasn't making it any easier for myself but I couldn't help it.

Soon after I retreated to my room there was a knock on my door and mum popped her head around, asking me if I wanted to talk. Even though I hadn't told her I was upset she knew. She always knew and as she tried to wipe the tears away I simply asked her, "Why? Why does it hurt me so much and Carl is fine?"

Handing me one of my favourite cakes she replied, "Only you can answer that, love. Do you know what it is that is upsetting you so much?"

"That is the problem, Mum, all of it upsets me. All of these questions I have running around in my head that I may not ever get the answer to. Thinking that I was a mistake and she gave me away, Mum it hurts. Do you think that she would be thinking about me today?"

"I have no doubt, my love. I know that you will always be in her heart, just like you are always in mine. I can't answer all your questions, darling, I wish I could, but you will understand one day that, I have no doubt, whatever her reasons were for placing you up for adoption, she did it out of love. Try and take some comfort from that."

"Mum, I love you so much and sometimes I feel bad that it bothers me so much, but you have always made it so easy for me to talk about."

"That is what I am here for, love, and you can always talk to me. One thing that you, or anybody else, won't ever have to reassure me about is that you are my daughter and you always will be. I am so grateful to Mary for doing what she did, as that is what brought us together. Mary is a part of your past, a very important part, and one day, hopefully, she will be part of our future too."

I nodded my head in agreement and then mum came up with an idea, "What if you were to write her letters, Mary, I mean?"

"What do you mean write her letters? I don't know where she lives and I am not allowed to find out?"

"You will have to use your imagination, love. I know you can't give them to her now, but what if every time you felt like this, instead of getting upset and coming up to your room, you could write her letters asking all of those questions you have and fill her in on everything happening in your life? It may be a good way of helping you cope."

"You always come up with the best ideas Mum. I think I would like that."

"Let's go downstairs then and I can make you some of my famous hot chocolate and we can think about how you would start."

And just like that she took me by the hand and we went back down the stairs, both smiling. Thinking back, that must have been so hard for my mum and even then, at my most insecure times, she still managed to give me comfort.

Minutes later mum rooted out a notepad and pen and I didn't waste any time getting started.

Dear Mary,

It's my birthday today! I am 13 years old. I think a lot about you on my birthday and it upsets me every year. Mum knew that I was upset today so she told me that I should write you letters, even though I will not be able to send them to you. Maybe you will get to read them some day. I hope so! I think it is a good idea as it helps me feel close to you. My mum and dad that adopted me are always so helpful when I get upset about being adopted. I love them very much and they are great but I don't think that anyone who isn't adopted can truly understand how confusing it is to be adopted. I have an older brother called Carl who is adopted also, but it doesn't seem to bother him the way it bothers me. I love my family but it is so confusing to think that I have a whole other family out there somewhere, but I don't know where?? I have so many questions to ask you, but for now I just hope you are ok.

Love Aoife

When I was growing up, some of my friends couldn't understand why I had such an interest in the woman who gave me away, especially since I had such an amazing family, but they didn't see that I never saw it as a reflection on my parents or brother, it just felt like a part of me was missing. When I was very young, mum would explain it to me and the one thing that sticks in my mind was her telling me that I was extra special, because I had two mums when most people only had one. She was so accepting of Mary's presence in my life, even though she wasn't physically present, and it was because of that, that I was able to make a decision that in my childish head seemed so simple.

I wanted to get to know my birth mother – whatever it took.

I have to say, I never felt resentful towards her, confused of course, but I was grateful for the life she gave me and sad that she had to make such a huge sacrifice. I see it that I'm so lucky she loved me enough to put me up for adoption. It is because of her that I had the life I ended up with. It must have been one of the most painful things any parent can experience.

I have an amazing supportive family and looking back through my childhood, I have nothing but happy memories. I always had so many people around me that loved and cared for me. We had family night every Friday, when dad would come home from work early and take us swimming at the local pool, and even though mum, conscious of her scars, never got into the pool she would never let that stop her from sitting on the water's edge, cheering us on.

On the way home every Friday we would get a take away and bring it home to the sitting room floor and play board games. Any new idea I came home with, like wanting to start ballet or horse riding, my folks would always bring me, spending a fortune on the right gear despite knowing that I would want to quit six months later.

I never used the excuse that I was adopted as a way out of anything, or because I was unhappy with certain aspects of my life. I was content.

Many of my friends weren't half as lucky as I was – but I still felt incomplete, I couldn't help it.

From the outside that must have seemed so ungrateful but I couldn't control it. I began to wonder what Mary's life was like. I had hoped she was OK and had gone on in life to have a husband and a family of her own, because even though Mary missed out on my childhood, I always wanted to share the memories of it with her. I never had a doubt in my mind that she loved me and even though I had never had contact with her, I felt her presence was always with me. It was only years later that I discovered how right I really was. I always knew (like an instinct inside me) that giving me up was the hardest thing she ever had to do. I knew we could never make up for the time lost, but it helped me to think that she would want to know how I grew up.

Like the first time our parents left Carl and me alone in the house for 30 minutes and we smashed the glass front door accidentally, playing chase, because he tried to lock me out. Or the time Amy and I decided to make a chocolate cake all on our own and everything from two large tins of cocoa powder to onion rings, flour and nuts went into it. We were so proud of our cooking skills but, of course, so sick from trying to eat it! There were summer nights spent playing tip the can on the road, the holidays with mum, dad and Carl driving up a mountain in Spain and fighting about who got to sit in the boot.

And then there was the winter it had snowed very heavily and we all decided we wanted to go to the park and race down the hills, so we all raided our houses to find something to make a good sleigh. I thought it would be a great idea to race down the hill on mum's new tray – burning a hole right through it in the process. Mum was not too impressed at the time.

Another great memory I have was when Clare, Katherine, Amy and I decided to make a newspaper for the road with all the gossip about the other kids.

All these memories were so important to me and I wanted to be able to share them with Mary someday. It really did help me to think that she would want to share these memories with me too, even if I was wrong. Mum was always a bit apprehensive when I would say that to her, because she knew over the years that the adoption agency had a lot of contact from Carl's birth mother, but never mine.

Not one word.

Amy

Growing up in Fonthill with the girls, was without a doubt the best childhood anyone could have hoped for. I moved there when I was two and my earliest memories are of playing with Aoife, Katherine and Clare on the road. We lived in a small private cul-de-sac with only 30 houses. Everybody knew each other and there was a wonderful closeness between all the families.

We were always so busy and active as kids. Aoife and I were very close as children, we practically lived in each other's pockets. We went to school together and we looked so alike that a lot of people often mistook us for sisters. We did ballet together, played camogie and often dressed up the same for Halloween – Aoife, of course, copied me!

Our parents were all so wonderful as well, especially Mr and Mrs Mac. They brought us everywhere and indulged all our childhhod whims. We were constantly having sleepovers in their living room, camping in their back garden and pretty much turning their house into our playground. We were extremely lucky children to have each other and to have such wonderful parents around us.

My brother and sister were also both adopted. My mum was told she was unable to have chidren so they adopted my sister and then my brother. Just after they were given my brother my mum was told she was pregnant! It must have been a very exciting and hectic time. Like Aoife's parents, mine were always very open with us about adoption and they explained carefully to us how some parents can't look after their children so they are given to a new mummy and daddy to look after them. There was never any difference between me and my siblings, we were treated the exact same and were like any other family.

I'm so happy for Aoife, Carl and my own sister and brother, that they grew up in such a loving and caring enviorment. I couldnt be prouder of Aoife and all she has acheived. Her strength and determination has always amazed me.

Mum worried about me when she knew how affected I was by being adopted. She knew how important it was for me to get some answers about my past and about where I came from but all she could do was wait with me, support me and hope that one day, when I did try to contact Mary, that her life would have turned out right for her and that she would want to meet me too. Mum and dad were always so secure in their role as parents that they were always supportive when I would talk about being adopted, or wanting to find my birth mother. I always felt like I could talk to them about it and when I would ask them if it bothered them that I wanted to find her they would just tell me, "not one little bit, it is the most natural thing in the world and of course you have questions. We will help you any way we can."

Mum knew, however, that the more time that passed the more I was struggling with the issue. As a young teenager it's hard to take in the complexity of the situation and I got a bit bogged down with the fact I was given up. I wasn't able to take it in at the time or to comprehend that Mary would have struggled so much with making that decision. I just couldn't see past the obvious. I couldn't see past all the questions, and one of the hardest parts was the not knowing. Not knowing if there was anyone in this world who looked like me. Not knowing anything about why she couldn't keep me.

I remember saying to mum over and over, "if I feel like this now how am I going to wait another three years, until I am 18, to even try and find out some more information?" And it was at this time that she asked me if I would think about going to talk to someone in the adoption agency. I knew they couldn't contact Mary, or even try to until I turned 18, but she thought it might help all the same.

I decided then, it was something I would like to do, especially when I found out that the adoption worker who I would be meeting with was the same lady that had dealt with Mary's case. Strange, I know, but I really wanted to meet someone, a real person, who had actually met my birth mother. I think at the time it was a way for me to feel connected to her.

Dear Mary,

I have been thinking loads about you this week. On Monday it
will be 15 years since we last saw each other. I hope the last 15
years have been good to you. I worry about you and how you
are. Monday will be my 15th birthday and these questions are
not getting any easier. Are you happy? Do you miss me? Have
you got any other kids? Why did you put me up for adoption?
Do you ever think about me? I don't know how I could miss
someone I have never known, but I feel like I do. How can I
know myself with such a big piece of the jigsaw missing? Mum
and dad got me a gorgeous ring for my birthday with my birth-
stone in it and we are going out for dinner too. They always
try and make my birthday special for me.

Love Aoife

Chapter 8 – More pieces of the puzzle

I GOT the bus into town that day on my own.

As I walked through the city centre I reminded myself of all the questions I wanted to ask and before I knew it I was at the big green door.

I wonder how many people feel like me knocking on this door I thought to myself as I waited for someone to answer.

"You must be Aoife, my name is Sarah, I am glad you found us ok, come on in," the lovely lady said as she led me into an office on the ground floor, that was surrounded on every wall with filing cabinets. It was a dark room that had a table in the middle. We sat down together in the centre of the room before Sarah looked at me with compassion and said, "Your mum has told me you're having a bit of a tough time at the minute, how do you think I could help you feel better?"

I knew it would be difficult expressing my feelings to a total stranger but I forced myself to quietly answer, "I don't know really. I know that there is nothing you can do but I am struggling with it all, especially when I think that it is going to be at least three more years before I can even begin to search for answers and even then I may not ever find any."

"You seem fairly determined for a fifteen-year-old."

"I feel like I have been waiting forever already and I have felt like this for as long as I can remember."

Once I stopped speaking Sarah looked at me and smiled, "It is amazing how much you look like her."

She then got up from her chair and went looking in one of the filing cabinets behind me without saying another word. I could feel the tears coming but was desperately trying to hold it together. *I look like her?* Such a small thing, but to me it meant everything. My racing thoughts were interrupted by Sarah returning with a file in her hand – Mary's file! She read through it silently for a few minutes. I think she must have been trying to be very careful as I was still underage and there was Mary's privacy to consider, so there wasn't much information she could tell me from it.

"Is there anything I need to worry about in there?" I asked.

"Not at all," she smiled.

"Let me see what I can tell you," she continued. "Mary lived at home when she was pregnant with you and she was a twin."

I was sitting on the edge of my seat trying to take in every word, while all of the time just wanting to grab this file out of her hands and devour it! It felt so unfair, this was my history, my past and they were keeping it from me.

Sarah continued, "She was unable to tell anyone about her pregnancy, even within her family, and she struggled a lot with the idea of putting you up for adoption but in the end she knew it was what was right for you because she could not give you the life that she wanted you to have."

I sat there as a huge sense of loss came over me, coupled with the realisation of how hard it must have been, how alone she must have felt at the time if she wasn't even able to confide in her twin. This made me feel sad.

Sarah thought to herself for a moment before asking me, "Would you like to know what she had called you?"

I raised my head from the floor, never having considered that she might have ever named me, and as quick as I could get the words out I responded, "Yes, I would love that."

"She called you Kathy."

Kathy

Just knowing that made me feel like I had an identity to her.

I was still chatting away to Sarah as she put the file back in one of the many cabinets, but just as she did a loud knock echoed through the hallway and she excused herself. I stared at those cabinets thinking, in that drawer, were the answers to so many of the questions I had always needed to know the answer to. It was a very strange feeling knowing that somebody else, a stranger, knew more about my past than I did but I stopped myself and tried to be content that I knew a lot more now than I ever had and I would have to be happy with that for now.

I couldn't wait to get home and tell my mum what I had found out. I know it sounds silly, but even little snippets of information helped me fill in some of the huge blanks I had about my past. I knew then for sure that Mary had struggled a lot with the situation. That she was trying to think of me too, and do what was right for me. It helped me knowing for sure that it wasn't just an easy way out she was looking for. That she was scared. I loved knowing that she had named me and even though this wasn't my name now, I felt connected to it. She loved me enough to give me a name and it meant so much.

When you don't know anything about the life that could have been yours, you are happy to take any little pieces you can get – even still, I wanted more.

*

Meeting the adoption worker really helped me get through the next few years. I now had some little pieces of the puzzle. It was a lot to take in as a teenager and looking back, I'm glad I was able to get bits and pieces of information gradually rather than all at once, even though I didn't feel like that at the time. I think it would have hit me like a tonne of bricks otherwise.

It was hard to understand when I was that young that life isn't black and white. That there are lots of grey areas and by learning little bits at a time it helped to take it all in. Still, at that time, all I can remember is counting down the years and months until my eighteenth birthday...

Dear Mary,

I thought this day would never come. Today is my 18th birthday. I have written another letter this week. It was to the adoption agency, asking them to help me find you. I am the most excited and the most terrified I have ever been in my whole life. I have never wanted anything as much as I have wanted to meet you. I need to meet you. PLEASE don't say NO. I understand facing your past is difficult but I'm not just the past. I'm here right now and I need you, need you to answer so many questions about who I am. I'm not angry and I never have been. I just need to know where I came from so that I can know me and I'm longing to know that you cared.

Love Aoife

I thought it would never come! I couldn't wait until I was able to try and unravel all of the unknowns that had surrounded my past and I found myself sitting in my room writing my long-awaited letter to the adoption agency, asking them to help in the search for my birth mother. For as long as I could remember I had looked forward to being able to write that letter. I just thought, maybe then, I could get some answers to the questions that had been burning inside me forever.

How did she walk out of that room and leave me there? Ignoring that maternal instinct I knew must have been screaming inside her. Did she ever think of me? Would she ever consider meeting me or even acknowledge that I was alive, to help me feel like my existence wasn't a complete mistake? Did I have any brothers or sisters? Did they know about me?

Is my birth mother even still alive?

Not having the answers that most people know and take for granted was very difficult to accept. I felt so much pain and confusion but I was so busy in my quest for knowledge that I never stopped to think of the real consequences, the personal effect and strain that posting that letter would have on me. I really had no idea what lay ahead or what to expect and I could never have of imagined that it would have been as hard as it was. It was such an emotional roller coaster and every part of my life had been affected. Now it was my turn to wait for the postman.

I received a letter back from the adoption agency not long after I had posted my first one. It simply said:

February 2000

Dear Aoife,

Thank you for your letter regarding your wish for us to assist you in tracing your birth mother. We would be pleased to help in any way possible. I am, however, required to inform you that at present we have a two-year waiting period before we could arrange a meeting with you as we are an extremely busy office and the demand at present exceeds our capabilities. We will be in touch again when your name has reached the top of our waiting list.

Regards,
Adoption worker

I was so upset. I had spent so long just waiting for my eighteenth birthday, I never thought past it. I had done all this waiting in order to just wait some more. I decided that day that I had to try my best to put it out of my mind. I would drive myself crazy if I didn't. I just had to get on with my life as best I could. I had no option.

It turned out to be good timing I guess. What eighteen-year-old isn't busy?! I had just finished school and started college. There were loads of nights out to be had with new and old friends. I was also working part-time in a local shop, while studying broadcasting and arts in Dun Laoghaire Institute of Art, Design and Technology.

It was a great couple of years and I was really coming into my own. I wasn't the most responsible girl in the world but I never really fully settled into school, I was quiet and shy for most of the time, so when I made some great new friends in college I was determined to enjoy every second of it. Not much studying and loads of parties – just the remedy I needed to keep my mind off the wait. I was young, single and for the first time since I could remember I was living in the moment, I was happy.

Before I knew it, the letter was dropped through my door:

41

This was it! I had been so busy enjoying college that I'd forgotten that those two years had felt like a life sentence when I first received the letter but now, it seemed, it had passed in a heartbeat.

All of a sudden it occurred to me though – over the years I had been so busy trying to get information and putting any little pieces of the puzzle together that I never stopped to think *what if*?

What if they can't find her?

What if she doesn't want to know anything about me?

What if she does?

What if she doesn't like me?

What if I don't like her?

What if I am rejected?

That's when the nerves came rushing at me.

Without warning I was so scared but then I was excited at same time.

Either way, I decided, nothing would keep me away from going to that meeting.

Dear Mary,

I have been waiting for so long to be told the waiting is over. I don't think I took the time to consider the reality of the situation. Yes, I need answers. I need answers so badly but what if, after all of these questions and all of this confusion, the only answer that I ever have is "No", you don't want to meet me? I finally have my appointment tomorrow to go and meet with the adoption agency. It has truly hit me for the first time, that even starting the process of trying to find you; I have to be so brave. I don't feel brave. I feel lost. How could something that I have wanted for so long be so scary to me?

Love Aoife

*

Taking the day off from college I walked through the city and got a coffee. I sat outside, under a canopy, just watching people dashing to get out of the rain with their umbrellas and briefcases over their heads. I was trying to get myself together before I opened that door and eventually I walked in the rain towards the adoption agency. I must have been the only person around not trying to keep dry – I had other things on my mind. Then I found myself at that big green door. My mind was going a mile a minute.

I must have been shaking when the adoption worker came to greet me but she just smiled and said warmly, "You must be Aoife. My name is Ann, and it is wonderful to finally meet you, come inside."

I was led into an office at the top of the building, right next to the room with the big windows overlooking the city. There was file after file piled high on this lady's desk and I finally understood the two-year waiting list. I could barely see where it ended!

I was just so glad, however, that my file was now on the top that I quietly and nervously sat in this room playing with my hair waiting for Ann to start speaking. I didn't know what to say.

"First of all, let me start by apologising about the delay in being able to meet with you. We are totally snowed under with reunions and searches and we simply cannot meet with the demand any sooner. I am sure the wait hasn't been easy for you?"

I smiled and replied, "I am just glad I am here now."

"Tell me a little bit about yourself and what has led you to want to search for your birth mother," Ann said.

43

She listened intently as I filled her in on stories from my childhood, my relationship with my parents and, most importantly, how adoption had affected my life. I saw pity in her eyes as she began to realise how important it was for me to find Mary.

"I was going to ask you next why you felt you wanted to search for your birth mother but already you have made it quite clear that this is something you have always felt you needed to do."

I smiled because I could tell that she got it. She got just how important this was to me and that made me feel comfortable.

"What are your expectations?" Ann continued.

"I don't really know to be honest. I haven't thought past finding her, meeting her. I just have so many questions and I guess my only real expectation is to do everything I can to understand. I want to hear from her how she felt and what happened."

Ann was jotting notes down while I was speaking, but I could tell she was listening to every word. I knew already she wanted to help me.

She took a moment before continuing.

"Not the nicest thing to ask but I need to ask you how would you cope if we couldn't find her, or if she didn't want you to find her?"

That was the one that left me stumped! *How would I cope if she didn't want to know me?*

I had spent so much time thinking about my birth mother over the years, and yes rejection came into my mind a bit, but how would I cope?

I wasn't sure I would and I didn't know how to answer so Ann continued, "Let me explain. The reason I asked you that question is that, unfortunately, not all searches are successful; or even when they are some birth mothers are not willing, for whatever reason, to reunite. Obviously we are hoping for the best possible outcome in your case, but I do need to prepare you for the fact that there are no certainties. I will be here for you every step of the way and I want you to understand that whatever the outcome you will not be going through this alone."

Ann gave me strength. She explained things so well, so I held my head high and replied, "I will try and deal with it if it happens, but I will never give up trying to find her. Until my birth mother herself says that she does not want contact with me I will keep trying. If it happens, and she is adamant, I will then put it to bed – but not until that day comes."

"I can see how determined you are," Ann smiled. "Have a think about everything we have discussed today. I know it is a lot to take in so write down any questions you have and we will meet again next week."

The last words she said to me, before I passed back through the green door, made me realise just how much Ann knew exactly how I felt.

"I know you have been waiting for this for so long, Aoife, so we will both be positive and take it one step at a time, together."

I walked back onto the street, that day, with a smile but also with so much to think about. Still I remained very clear about what I wanted and was also so relieved that Ann was so respectful of my wishes. I knew she wanted things to work out for me and I was so glad to have her in my corner.

*

The second meeting I had with Ann was pretty similar to the first. I was full of joy, mixed with nerves and excitement, as she explained to me how things were going to proceed and how they would attempt to find my birth mother. She said that they had to be very careful in how they went about things in order to protect my birth mother's right to privacy. They had no idea about her life now, or if, twenty years later, anyone in her life even knew about me, and if it was the case that they did not, then they could not be the ones to expose her secret. Ann said that once they had found an address for Mary (which could take some time) that they would write her a letter that didn't give too much away, but on which she would hopefully read between the lines. After that they hoped she would get in touch with them. One thing was for sure, they couldn't risk saying anything in the letter about "the child that she gave up for adoption" in case it was read by somebody else.

As I sat there I was thinking that it was all very vague, but I trusted the adoption agency and their knowledge and experience – most importantly I trusted Ann. This was obviously a process that had worked for them in the past and she had made it clear from the beginning that she would do anything in her power to help me find closure, so I was satisfied.
I needed their help and support in tracing my birth mother and I was prepared to do it any way they wanted me to.

It was all so exciting. I finally felt like I was getting the ball rolling. Finally I was allowed to start my search. I had been waiting my whole life for this and now it was real. I tried really hard to stay grounded and not let my mind run away from me with all the "*what ifs*" – the ones that had been plaguing me for years. I had to try and remind myself that although it was all very exciting, it could all end just as fast as it had begun.

At this stage I was beginning to understand why they make you wait so long to get information, or attempt to search for any birth parents. It is so much to take in and you have to be prepared for any scenario. I guess, in a way, you have to prepare yourself for the fact that you may be rejected all over again too, and that is one of the hardest parts.

I had wanted to do this my entire life, but I would be lying if I said that during the emotional roller coaster that was the search, I didn't second guess what I was putting myself through, many times.

I thought that the day the adoption agency told me they were going to start and attempt to trace Mary, that it was the end of my journey, the end of the waiting. Little did I know that it was only the beginning!

*

Not much time had passed after my second meeting at the adoption agency when I received a phone call. I was in the middle of a broadcast recording in college, for the radio show we were working on, when I looked at my phone and my heart skipped a beat. It was the adoption agency. I wasn't expecting a call from them so soon. They had explained to me over and over that it would probably take some time before they had any news at all and it was only at my second meeting that they had told me that they were officially starting the search. *Could they possibly have news already? What if it was bad news?* These questions raced through my mind in the few seconds before I answered my phone, after quickly showing the screen to my college friend Brid, and racing out of the studio.

"Hello?"

"Hi, Aoife, it's Ann here. I just wanted to give you a quick update. After we last spoke I sent a letter to the only address we have for Mary, in the hope she or a family member may still be there. When we had no response from that I was, again, looking through Mary's file and noticed that there was also a contact phone number, so I phoned it this morning. We have a bit of a way to go, but I did find out some information that I thought you would be eager to hear."

My heart felt as though it might burst through my chest in anticipation. "That's amazing, I would love to hear. What did you find?"

"I was speaking to Mary's mother this morning, she still lives at the family home. I was careful not to divulge the reason for my call, I simply said I was an old friend of Mary's and was looking to reconnect with her if her mother could possibly help out. She was very friendly and immediately gave me Mary's current address and phone number. She also told me that Mary lives with her husband now."

I couldn't believe our luck. She was alive for a start! And she was married... all of those years hoping she was OK – now I knew she was! The relief was overwhelming, but I managed to stay composed.

"Every bit of progress, Ann, is getting us a step closer, thank you so much for calling. It's the best news. What happens now?"

"We still have to consider Mary's privacy, so a letter has gone out to her address today and we will take it from there."

"Thanks again, Ann, keep me posted please."

I know it was only little snippets of information about her, but considering I previously knew very little about Mary, any little piece of the puzzle was an amazing feeling. I now knew the answer to a few more of the questions that had built up over the years. I knew that she was living in the country, living in Dublin. I now knew that she had got married. I was happy about that. I also knew that the kind lady on the phone to the adoption worker was my grandmother. Wow! It was an amazing feeling. I couldn't believe it was all happening. Finally! I also knew that by the end of the week Mary would have a letter sent to her and all I had to do now was wait.

What I didn't know was for how long…

> Dear Mary,
>
> It must be around twenty years since we last met. I hope you are keeping well. I have recently met up with Kathy on a number of occasions and we are hoping to organise a college reunion. I would be very grateful if, when you receive this letter, that you contact me.
>
> Regards,
> Ann

Ann was hoping that because Mary had named me Kathy when I was born, and she said it had been twenty years since they last saw each other, Mary would realise that it was actually me she was taking about, and call the office.

When Ann was given Mary's address she also informed me she "doesn't live a million miles away from you". She gave me the impression, without actually telling me, that she lived very close to me and, to be honest, that really messed with my head. It is a very strange feeling being in your comfort zone, your hometown, yet walking past a stranger and thinking, *could she be my natural mother?* After that I began to think to myself, *how many times have I walked past her on the street and not known who she was?"*
It really shocked me to think it was actually possible to have seen her before, as a teenager, as an adult… it made it all feel so real. Until then, it was hard for me to really comprehend the reality of the situation. It had been like a story I had always been told about somebody and their life, like a fairy tale I grew up hearing, but I never really expected to see the seven dwarfs walking down the street holding Snow White's hand. After the day that I found out she was living close to me, I found myself looking at every lady I saw around that age, or similar to me, and thinking, *are you my mother?* I wasn't able to concentrate on anything else and all the waiting was really beginning to

take its toll. Every day seemed like a week and all I found myself doing was waiting for the phone to ring – waiting for the call I began to think wasn't coming…

After the initial excitement, I found going to the meetings with Ann more difficult and they got harder each time. Every time I knocked on that green door and was led into the office at the back I was expecting her to have news for me, but each time there was nothing, and I felt a little more crushed.

Mary hadn't responded to the letter and I couldn't understand why they would not just phone her. I knew they had got her number, but when I would ask them that, they would tell me that they would write to her again, that a letter was better because if they phoned her and I was still a secret, that she might not be alone and it could cause her trouble – even be too much of a shock.

I did understand their point, but it was getting so hard to be patient. In hindsight they were trying to prepare me for the fact that Mary was ignoring the letters and that I could have to accept that she might not want contact. But I could not do that! Not until they had spoken to her and the words had come out of her mouth. The ones that stated, without doubt, that she didn't want contact with me. I was holding on to the hope that maybe she didn't understand what the letter meant. The alternative, that I was being rejected all over again, was too hard to accept. If what I grew up thinking was true, that giving me up was the hardest thing she ever had to do and that she was doing it for me, then why was she rejecting me now? I began to try and look at things from her point of view and I did understand that it must be so difficult dragging up the past. She didn't really owe me anything twenty years on and I knew that in order for anyone to get over giving up a child, that in order to deal with the pain, they would have to block out a lot and try to fully move on with their life. It was a very hard time for me as each meeting with the adoption agency just left me feeling sad, alone and confused.

I had to remind myself, however, that I had said I'd never give up, not until I absolutely knew, and that is what got me though the weeks that turned into months. The only thing I thought I did deserve from her, either way, was an answer. Then I could accept things and move on – without it I couldn't. I couldn't handle any more unknowns. My whole life had been full of them. I needed closure but I began to think, after two or three letters were sent, that she was ignoring them and I began to feel resentful towards her. I felt like she wasn't even acknowledging that I was alive. Ignoring the fact that I even existed and when I would ask the adoption agency if there was any way she just didn't understand what the letter was regarding they would tell me no. She would know. So they didn't give me any hope to cling on to.

My first meeting with the adoption agency had been April 23rd.
It was now August and still nothing...

Chapter 9 – If one door closes, find a window

RIGHT, a bit of advice. Get active!

If you find yourself in a situation that is difficult to deal with, whatever it may be, then try and adapt to the situation. Change it into something you find easier. That is exactly what I did. I wasn't going to give up, I decided, I was going to change my actions. How I was conducting myself was the only thing in the situation, over which I had any control. My actions! Most of which, so far, had been waiting. Waiting for the phone to ring and letting my imagination run away with me. So I was going to do something positive, for me. I was going to try and find Mary myself.

No more waiting about doing nothing, in limbo, and not knowing anything. Although the adoption agency had found Mary, because they had known her original address, I had not got access to any of that information. All I knew was what I had always known and that she was married – that's where it ended. So I gathered all my information together and this is what I had:

My birth mother was 24 when I was born. Her first name is Mary and she is a twin. She had given birth to me in Holles Street hospital on the 10/02/1982 and called me Kathy.

So how was I going to use this information? It wasn't much to go on and Dublin is a big city. Admittedly, I didn't know what I was going to do yet. I didn't even know what I *would* do if I did find her – it's not like I could have just turned up on her doorstep and said, "Hi, I'm your daughter." I do know, however, that having just made the decision to be proactive in finding her myself helped me to feel useful, and I was just going to take it one step at a time. Where there is a will there is always a way, as I kept reminding myself.

Eventually I spoke to my dad about what I was thinking and how I was feeling, and as he always has been, he was right there for me. He told me that he would help in any way he could and so, without wasting another second, we took to the internet. After hours and hours of trawling, looking for anything we could connect to her, we decided our next step would be to use public information. My dad had some experience tracing people back through history for a family tree he had been working on, so he knew the process. This time, however, he had very little information to work with, but we decided we would give it a go all the same. Dad took the day off work and we went to the place where all the public births, deaths and marriage certificates are kept in Dublin. Our first stop was to look at all the births the year I was born. Arriving at Lombard Street that day I couldn't wait to get started, but I was scared too – scared of what I would find. Scared of what I wouldn't find, but the only way I was going to know for sure was by getting stuck in so we walked into the building more determined than ever that we would find something, anything that would help in my quest. Even a small piece of the puzzle would do.

The office we were looking for was on the first floor. I nearly ran up the stairs I was so eager to get started. To the left was a reception desk with rows and rows of register books that were piled up to the ceiling behind it. There were tables and chairs set out in front, for people to search through the registers; and 10 or so people were already sitting, scanning the pages of huge books.

"Where do we start?" I asked dad.

"One book at a time, Aoife, one book at a time."

After coming up with a game plan we got to work. Looking at the size of each one of these entry books made the whole process seem so overwhelming and it proved a long day but, we thought, if we looked at all the births on the year I was born, we would also find all the births in Holles Street hospital on that day. We passed the time by talking about Mary and when I was first adopted by mum and dad.

"Do you remember the day I came home Dad?"

"Like it was yesterday," he replied with a smile. "I was so excited to find out I was going to have a daughter, even if we did dress you in Carl's old blue babygrows for the first six months! I think when we started to dress you in pink people were shocked you were a girl at all," he laughed.

"Today must be hard for you, but Dad I couldn't have even tried to do this without you."

"You are not to worry about how mum or I feel Aoife. We know you are our daughter and nothing will change that, but Mary is a part of the reason you are our daughter and if we can manage to find her we would welcome her to be a part of our family too. I want to meet her nearly as much as you do. We have a big thank you, that we would love to have the opportunity to say to her."

He thought then for a second and, with raised eyebrows, added. "Maybe you got your impulsive personality from her."

I laughed then too, because he was right. Unlike my parents I had always been the type to jump in feet first – and sometimes with my eyes closed – whereas mum and dad didn't make any decision without thinking it out, talking it through and weighing up all the options. This infuriated me at times, as I am sure my impulsiveness did them – we were like chalk and cheese in that regard. I guess, however, that I needed their level heads to stop myself making bigger mistakes in life.

The sound of my father's voice again, brought me back to reality.

"Right, come here for a second Aoife, I have found the first birth in Holles street on the day you were born, let me show you how we can narrow it down. Look for the entry of the mother's maiden name, if it is not Mary move on, and if it is we are on the right track."

"OK, then what?" I eagerly replied.

"Then we are looking for what name they called their child. If it is Kathy then it might be you so we will have to flag it."

There were a few Marys and a couple of Kathys and by the time we were finished, I realised, I would know that one of these two women was my birth mother! But how would we find out which one? I was stuck but dad didn't waste much time before he figured it out.

"We are getting close now, it's really getting exciting," he said. "If we go and look back to the year our Mary was born one of these ladies should be ruled out and then we will know."

My Mary was 24 but when a person looks up the register book in that office, it is only the short form of everything they will see. So each time we thought we had a match to something, we had to go up to the lady at the reception, pay a small fee and request the long form in order to get the information we needed.

We kept our heads down though, and got on with the job in hand. Eventually we got the two birth certificates of the two Kathys born on the 10th of February. They obviously had Mary's name on them so we looked up the year my Mary would have been born, to see if we could find out if one of the Marys was born that year, making her 24 years old, on the day I was born. We then requested the long form birth certificate thinking *this is it! We are so close to finding out who my birth mother is.* But we were suddenly stopped in our tracks…

"Sorry we are closing. We can't look up that information for you today," said the lady behind the counter.

I was inconsolable. We were so close and I really felt that I just couldn't wait one more minute, let alone another day longer after all the waiting I had already done. I had no choice, however, but to accept defeat for the day. Before we left, however, the receptionist looked at me over her glasses, and with a smile she told us that she would look it up first thing in the morning and send it out to us in the post. We had no other option, so with my head in my hands, we returned home and waited for the postman!

Two days passed and he finally came. My heart was racing. *Will this be it?* I wondered. *Will I finally know who my birth mother is?*

We had a match! One of the Marys that had her baby in Holles Street hospital on the 10th of February, 1982 was 24 at the time of my birth. *Was this my birth mother? Had I found that information myself? How could I be sure?* Then I noticed a column to the side where it said Mary's full name as child, her parent's names below and a line that said she was a twin. There it was, the confirmation that I was looking for! This was Mary, my birth mother, and I was looking right at her birth certificate. Now, how did I know where to go from here?

Dad.

Again we began going over what information we had gathered, full of excitement about our most recent find, and we asked ourselves what we were going to do next. How would we use this information to find Mary? There was an address, on the birth certificate, of where her parents had been living at the time of her birth. I assumed that could have still been her mother's address. Maybe it was her old family home? But I couldn't use that to find her as I thought it was only right to speak only to her, in case she hadn't told anyone about me.

Still, more and more pieces of my life puzzle were again coming together. Dad and I sat down that night and we had decided that one more trip into the registration office was needed. We knew that we had found the right Mary, and her full name, something I had never known; but I had also been told from the adoption agency that she was married. The chances were that she had probably changed her name to her married name at some stage over the years. We had more hurdles to jump, but we had come so far and I now had the energy and excitement to face them head on.

If one door closes, look for a window!

Back at the registration office for the second time, we were now on the hunt for Mary's marriage certificate. This one, however, wasn't as straightforward as the last. For some reason, at that time, only marriages up to 1995 were held in that office. Anything after that was held in some office down the country, which wasn't open to the public to sift through. So this meant I had a window. I hoped she had been married sometime on or before 1995, because otherwise my search stopped right there. I couldn't find her myself if I didn't know her married name.

I was very nervous that day, but the mountain of information we had to go through kept me busy. I found my own table to sit at, in the corner of the room by a window. Hour after hour passed as I scanned the pages of those huge books with the noise of the busy street below filtering into the room;

but with each one I finished I noticed the sun moving further along from one side of the floor to the other. It was coming to the end of the day and the office was closing. I started to feel panicky but as I rushed through the last year of records, 1995, I heard a sudden shriek from my dad.

"I have it!"

The very last year and he had found it! We now had one of the last pieces of information that we needed – her married name and her husband's name. I was elated and followed dad's gaze towards the corner of the room where, sitting on a tall table, was a phone book. We then looked at each other and he said, "You never know, we'll give it a go."

At that time, her married name was unusual, so there was not that many of them in the phone book. My dad looked it up, I hadn't got the heart to, because if she wasn't listed there it simply meant one thing – I would have to place all of my hope for a reunion back in the hands of the adoption agency.

After a minute or so of scanning the page, however, dad looked at me and smiled and I knew he had it. Her name and her husband's were listed together in a place that was a five-minute drive from our own house!

I was speechless, overcome with emotion, and as I looked at my dad I thought I would burst with love for him. My amazing, kind, caring father had just found my birth mother and in doing so had given me the most selfless, important gift I would ever receive.

There were no words needed as the man who did just what this lady couldn't, and raised me with love, support and compassion, leaned over and hugged me with all his might. I felt I could never repay him.

As we walked from the office it slowly dawned on me that if I'd had this brainwave earlier, technically I could have found her at any time over the previous years. I am glad, now, though that I didn't because I didn't know it at the time, but you have to be emotionally ready for the roller coaster ride and even then it is hard. I don't think I would have coped too well if I was just a couple of years younger – it really does take a lot out of you – and you can never forget the possibility that you could be rejected. I needed to remind myself of that every step of the way, to emotionally prepare myself for it, because if I didn't it would have been too far to fall at the end of it all.

Having found Mary's address I couldn't hold my excitement back. It was an amazing feeling and my dad and I left the registers office in shock that she had been so near to us all this time... I had heard of six degrees of separation but this was crazy! Driving home we couldn't stop smiling when we noticed a sign that pointed in the direction of where she lived, and after a millisecond we looked at each other and said, "Let's just go see!"

At that stage I really wanted to see where she was living. I wasn't going to do anything and besides, even though I know my dad would never have admitted it to me, it was hard for him and I did not want to push it. There were times, throughout my search, that I felt lost and confused – times I felt rejected, believing that she wouldn't want to know me; but thanks to this amazing man constantly by my side I never ever felt alone.

We drove into the estate and all the way to the back, taking in all the surroundings. There were children playing on a green as we drove by and people out cutting their grass. It looked like a lovely place to live. When we got close to where I thought the house was, I kept busy concentrating on the numbers so we could drive by the one she lived in.

"What numbers are on that side Dad?"

"I think it will be coming up on the left so I will drive slowly."

And all of a sudden it was there and I didn't have time to even take in the fact that this was my birth mother's home, to comprehend that this had been the closest I had ever got to her; because almost immediately my eyes were drawn to the car in the driveway and the lady getting out of it.

My heart must have stopped beating, as the sweat formed on my forehead and I began to choke up.

"Oh my God, Dad, there is someone there!"

Our car was still moving slowly when she turned around to shut her own car door. It was her! I just knew immediately that it was my birth mother I was looking at.

"Dad, seriously that is her, I know it is her." I could see myself in her. Dad handed me a tissue to wipe away the tears from my eyes.

"Oh dear I wasn't expecting this, what do you want me to do, love?"

I couldn't take my eyes off her and then her front door opened before I could answer. A little boy raced from it and into her arms, welcoming her home. *Was this my little brother?*

"Drive, Dad, I have to get out of here, it's too much!"

"I will just move down here to the end of the cul-de-sac and you can decide what to do," he replied.

"I'm not ready to meet her. I wasn't even ready to see her" I blubbered through my tissue. "I've waited so long for this, how can I not be ready? But I'm not, Dad. I want to go home, please just bring me home."

I knew we had to drive past the house again in order to get out of the estate and I could barely breathe. I couldn't think. I just cried. I was so close to the end of this long road, so close to possibly meeting her, yet still so close to the possibility of rejection. Now it was real like never before and it was too much for me to deal with.

With all of these thoughts racing through my mind, dad came near to the entrance of the estate and pulled the car over and said, "Don't panic Aoife, of course you feel all of these things, I don't think either of us expected her to be standing there. I mean, come on, what are the odds of that?" He couldn't help but laugh while giving me a reassuring hug. "Calm down for a second and let's think. Are you OK, love?"

"Yeah, I'm OK Dad," I just about managed to get the words out. "I think I just got a shock, I have wanted this for so long, but why, when it happened, did I just want to run away?"

His kind eyes, the ones I was so familiar with, made me relax a little as he answered. "That is perfectly normal. Remember you were not expecting to see her, and you would have to prepare yourself for that."

With the mention of preparation thoughts of the adoption agency entered my head and I gasped as I said, "Oh God, I haven't told the adoption agency that I have been trying to find her myself, because I knew they would not approve and would try to talk me out of it. Dad, what will I do?"

I was panicking again. I had to tell them now! I needed their help!

Dad smiled, taking the whole situation in his stride, and handed me his phone before saying, "There is no time like the present."

We sat in the car at the side of the road and, still shaking, I dialled Ann's number.

When she answered I started speaking at a mile a minute, feeling very much like a lost little girl who had just done something wrong and was afraid to confess. I don't even know how I got the words out but I knew it was now or never so as soon as I got the opportunity I blurted out, "I have found my birth mother myself and I have just seen her…"

I think I was afraid to wait for her reaction so I continued on before she had a chance to say a word, explaining that I just couldn't handle waiting for any more letters to be sent.

"Mary is home now!" I was practically shouting. "She is in her house now! Will you please phone her?"

It didn't take anything more. Ann heard the urgency in my voice, so she agreed. She didn't react negatively at all and to this day I still don't know why. Was it that she knew I wasn't coping with not having an answer, or was it because she was afraid I would knock on her door? Either way, she agreed and told me she would phone me back.

That was the 10th of September 2002. Little did I know it would be the day that would change the rest of my life…

Dad

"I will always remember something which happened about 40 years ago. My mother and I were home on a bright sunny day on a rug in the back garden. My cousin and his wife arrived unexpectedly with a baby they had just got the previous day, which they were going to adopt. My cousin was an only

child and his father had died when he was seven, so he spent a lot of time with our family and was more like a brother than a cousin. The joy of that occasion was palpable and I will never forget it.

On my father's side of the family my cousin, who lived on the farm which my father referred to as home, had two adopted children. My wife's brother had three children, the eldest of which was adopted. On the road we lived on our neighbour had an adopted child and another had two adopted children – so adoption was quite normal as far as we were concerned. We were lucky enough to be able to adopt two children and we were advised that children who were adopted should know at an early age that they are adopted – even though they wouldn't actually know what it meant until they were much older.

Aoife always had a curiosity about her birth mother. We saw this as quite natural (particularly for a girl) and when she was old enough we contacted the adoption agency to try and help her find her birth mother. The right place to start any such search was through the adoption agency. It was hard to see Aoife become increasingly upset [when there was no progress] and I would have done anything to help.

After all of the research was done and Aoife and I found ourselves in Mary's estate driving to see where she lived I think I was as excited as she was. It was a mystery that had gone unsolved for years, causing my daughter a lot of pain, and it felt good helping her. I was caught up in the excitement and Aoife realised before I did, when we passed by the house Mary was living in, that there was actually somebody standing in the driveway. Aoife was in a state of shock. So was I to be honest. I pulled the car over to the side of the road, away from Mary's house, and Aoife phoned the adoption agency. Maybe this time our research was too successful, but I was glad I was there to help."

*

When we got home that day dad put the kettle on and I sat down with mum in the kitchen to tell her everything that had happened. She couldn't believe it but she was more in shock at my normally level-headed dad who had given in to my impulsiveness! But that didn't matter. What mattered was that we found Mary and I think mum was just relieved that I had decided to contact the adoption agency and not speak to her myself. Rejection face to face would have been a whole other story.

After I had told my mum everything I decided to go for a walk. It was so difficult to get things clear in my head. This was no longer a fairy tale story, it was a reality. Mary was a real person who lived in a real house and had a real little boy.

I walked and walked, not even noticing that it had started to rain, but my train of thought was soon interrupted by my phone ringing. I took it out of my pocket and I looked at the screen. It was the adoption agency! It had only been an hour since I had phoned Ann.

Why would she be phoning me again so soon?

Again I got that feeling that I couldn't breathe. Time stood still for a moment. I just knew this was the phone call that would finally give me my answer. Whether or not it was the answer I had been hoping for I did not know, but either way it was about to be cleared up. Wiping the rain away from the screen with my hand shaking, I answered the phone.

"Hello, Aoife, it's Ann. I have finally got some good news for you!"

Ann had got through to Mary. She had only put the phone down from speaking to her and she called me straight away. She immediately told me that Mary hadn't realised who had been sending her the letters and she said that she had not realised that it was me who was trying to contact her.

"Mary got very emotional, but she didn't hesitate when I asked her if she would consider meeting you, Aoife. She immediately said that YES, SHE 100% WANTED TO MEET YOU. She had no clue who had been writing her letters for months, so this was a huge shock for her too."

Mary had filled Ann in on bits of her life. She still had never told anyone about giving a child up for adoption, but she had told Ann that nothing would stop her meeting me and she would finally now tell her family as she felt the time was right.

That was also the day that I first heard that I had a half brother and sister. Mary told Ann that she went on to get married and had two children that were now 6 and 4 years old. This was amazing! I think I must have been numb at first. So many times I had answered the phone to Ann expecting to hear good news, only to be disappointed.

Now she was telling me everything I had longed to hear.

I stopped walking and sat down on a wall beside a river, just staring into the water. I don't even think I was paying much attention to the rest of the conversation. *Mary wanted to meet me! Was this really happening? I wasn't being rejected! I was wanted! She wanted to meet me…*

I don't think I have ever experienced a feeling like it in my life. I didn't know what to do. Such a mix of emotions all at once! All I knew was that I needed my mum. She was my rock. She always knew what to do and no one else could understand like she did. She had been there for every step of my journey and I knew I had to get myself together and go home to her.

We talked about what was going to happen for ages that evening and I asked mum for the millionth time if she was OK with all of it. As usual she simply smiled and said, "I have always been secure in our relationship and it is the most natural thing in the world."

"Mum, can you come with me when I go to meet her? I need to understand, but I don't think I can do it on my own."

"You will never have to do anything like that on your own, love, of course I will go with you. We are all in this together," she replied with a smile.

Dear Mary,

It is so hard to comprehend that I am writing you a letter that you are actually going to read. After all the years of questions racing around my head, after the countless letters I have written to you over the years, knowing that I could never send them, it is now a reality. The reality that you were eager to have contact with me! After all that, I now don't know what to write. My biggest fear with all of this was that I would never have contact with you. That you would say no and walk away! Thank you so much for facing your past for me. I had a great childhood and that is all down to my parents and my brother. I know how lucky I have been that I grew up with so much love and support. They are all supporting me 100% in my contact with you too. I am in college at the minute and loving the social life. I hope you are happy in your life. I am very much looking forward to meeting you.

Love Aoife

Ann had asked me to come in and speak to her the next day, to have a chat about the next step. It was so important that we didn't rush in, and that we handled the situation properly. I have never found it so difficult to be patient! I was bursting to meet her, but considering my reaction when I saw her for the first time, I was happy to follow Ann's instructions now.

Ann wanted it to sink in for us both first. She wanted to have a couple of preparation meetings with me first and a couple of preparation meetings with Mary also.

And so I walked through the city that day thinking to myself that soon I would be making the journey to meet my birth mother for the first time. Soon, the questions that I'd had, the unknowns I'd had all my life, would be answered. Again I knocked on that big green door, with a huge smile on my face this time, to meet Ann. She opened the door and greeted me with the same smile she always did before leading me into the office at the back. She was holding a letter in her hands. I noticed it straight away and my impulsive, impatient personality kicked into gear. I wanted to grab it out of her hands, but she didn't make reference to it at first. We sat down and she told me she had met Mary.

She had come in to see her that morning, because ever since she received the initial phone call and realised it was me who had been trying to contact her, she was very keen to get the ball rolling. I smiled to myself, remembering dad's comment about my impatient personality. Maybe I did get that side of me from Mary!

Ann told me that Mary was very eager for me to know that she wanted to meet me as soon as possible and was upset at the thought that I had been trying to contact her for months and she didn't know. She was upset that I must have felt rejected. For the second time in my life I was told that day, that Mary and I looked alike but more than that – we had the same eyes and were the same height. Ann said that Mary was a lovely lady who was very much looking forward to meeting me.

It was so hard to take in. *My birth mother was looking forward to meeting me!*

I don't know if even after all my searches, that I believed it would really happen. But I think now, knowing what I know, that it was fate. Ann went on to tell me that Mary hadn't told anyone in her family about me. Her twin sister or her husband still did not know that I ever existed. That at the time I was born, she tried to block it out. It was too painful to think of anybody else looking after her baby, even though she did know it was the right decision for me. She informed Ann, however, that she was now going to tell her family that she had a daughter and even though I didn't know her yet, I felt proud of her.

After keeping a secret so big, for so long, that was going to be difficult.

I talked for nearly an hour with Ann that day, teasing any piece of information I could get out of her.

Eventually she looked down to the hand that was holding the letter and told me it was for me. Mary had written it. I have never been so excited to read words on a page before. Ann said it was a good idea if Mary and I wrote to each other first, before we met, in order to get to know each other a little bit before the big day.

Ann passed me the letter and I left through the big green door once more.

My dearest Aoife,

Words cannot express the emotion I felt when I got the call about you searching for me. It has been so emotional for me reliving the past and there is so much I want to say. Firstly if I had any idea, at all, that those letters were from you I would have replied straight away. The silence must have been so difficult for you. I never connected them to you at all. I drove to the park after I got the phone call from Ann and sat there for hours reliving the time you were adopted. It brings me so much joy to finally hear that you were adopted into an amazing family. Somehow all the years I spent worrying that you were OK, happy and safe, came flooding back. I still have a lot to work out emotionally but I really cannot wait to meet you and thank you so much for taking that first step. I am married now and I have two children. I need to tell you that I have not told any of them yet but nothing is going to stop me from telling them now.
We have a lifetime to catch up on.

With all my love,
Mary

I must have read that letter 100 times. I could not wait to write back to her. I wanted her to know that I was fine, I had amazing supportive parents who were supporting me through this too, and she didn't have to rush to tell anyone until she was ready. I knew how much of a big deal it was and I didn't want to put pressure on her. I filled in some more blanks about my life and I told her that I could not wait to meet her. The next letter I received, through Ann, from Mary, was amazing. She couldn't have done anything else to make me feel more accepted.

My dearest Aoife,

I could not wait another minute before writing to you. The secret that I had buried for so many years is a secret no more. I felt an overwhelming sense of guilt as I wrote you that first letter and then saw the words written on the page – that I had not told anyone of your existence. You have been in my heart since the day you were born and as soon as I knew you wanted to meet me I couldn't keep that secret any longer. I told Mick, my husband, first and I have to admit I was terrified. I was shocked when he was so loving, so supportive of me. I should have known he would be but my secret built up in my head for so long that it became too big to handle, if that makes sense. Mick and I told the children together that night, during a bedtime story, and they are so excited, they cannot wait to meet their big sister.

There is so much excitement around the house.

With all my love,
Mary.

Their big sister! Wow! This was more than I had ever dreamed of. Not only my birth mother, but also her family wanted a relationship with me.

I had waited twenty years to meet her, but never in my wildest dreams did I think that they would all accept me into their lives like this.

I had never expected it and had to pinch myself.

Was this too good to be true? Was I dreaming?

I was still trying to take it all in when I realised that there was more pages to the letter. I turned one over and on it were hand written notes. On each one a different person was welcoming me to the family. They were letters from Mary's husband, her two kids and aunts and uncles.

Dear Aoife,

What a day!

It is Mick here, Mary's husband. We are all here sitting around the kitchen table celebrating your arrival into our family. Mary has been very emotional and I have to admit I have shed a few tears. We are all so excited to meet you.

Dear Aoife,
We are so happy that we have a new big sister. Mum and Dad told us we can meet you soon and we can't wait. We are six and four.

Dear Aoife,

Wow! What can we say, welcome to the family. We have all spent the evening here with Mary listening to all the news about you and toasting you with champagne. We can't wait to share a glass with you. We are planning a party already for the day we get to meet you and everybody is so excited. We have seen your picture and we are all shocked at how much you look like Mary. Thinking back we can't believe we never knew about you, but we are all so happy for you and Mary, that we know now.

Welcome to the family.

All your Aunts and Uncles.

The few minutes I was reading them felt like I was looking in on someone else's life. It didn't feel real. Mary and her husband had invited the rest of their family over and she told them all about me, after which they all welcomed the news with open arms! They were there to support Mary, who had been alone, scared and carrying this secret for so long by herself. They took the weight off her shoulders. That is what family is all about. I had the support of a loving family throughout my life and I was so glad to now know that she had the support of a loving family in her life also. None of them knew me and still they were, just like that, welcoming me into their family.

I couldn't reply to each of them quickly enough and at that stage I could barely contain my excitement. There was no more fear of rejection. It was that one letter that lifted it right off my shoulders. I finally felt like everything would work out.

All the while though, Ann was trying to keep Mary and me cautious. She wanted us both to realise, that even when people really want to reunite, they shouldn't assume that the relationship will work out, because they might decide they are too different and not stay in touch.

I don't think I had ever felt so much excitement during the time Mary and I were writing to each other. I let go of all of my fears because I knew she wasn't rejecting me. Eventually, however, I did begin to realise that I should listen to Ann's advice. I had to come back down to earth and remind myself that it could go any way. I felt like I knew things would work out, but at the end of the day, how did I really know?

Was I just dragging myself back into a fairy tale after only reading the first few pages of our journey together and writing a happy-ever-after ending in my head? As hard as it was, I had to force myself not to get carried away. Mary had no idea what type of a person I was and I had no idea what type of a person she was and there were still so many questions I could only ask her in person. *What if I didn't like the answers?* The fear was beginning to creep back into my mind and I just kept saying, over and over to myself, *This is really happening, but take it slow.* I had one chance to make this right, so I had to just relax, be myself and have an open mind.

I had given the letter responding to Mary and her family to Ann, just like we had both done before and Ann would usually inform me that she had another letter from Mary, and I would go in and collect it. But not this time!

The next time the phone rang Ann had a different message…

*

There had been a lot of contact with her over the previous days and weeks, so I didn't get the panicky feeling when I saw Ann's number flash on my phone anymore. I had been chatting for a couple of minutes with her, as she asked me how I was feeling about everything that had happened and if I was coping OK, when, satisfied with my answers, she finally said the words I had been waiting for.

"Mary wants to meet you as soon as possible!"

I was stunned into momentary silence as Ann explained that Mary had received the letters I had sent back to her and that she felt it was now time for us to meet face to face. There it was again… that panicky feeling! I couldn't breathe and it took all of my courage to get the words out and reply, "Yes, I feel ready to meet too."

My whole life had been a roller coaster of emotions in relation to adoption and this was probably the peak of it. It was all very confusing. I knew I wanted to meet Mary more than anything, but I was terrified and excited too. I wanted to run away, but I wanted to run to her at the same time.

I just needed courage now to follow through with it.

*

Reuniting a birth mother and child isn't a straightforward process and every little detail needs to be precisely planned, prepared and organised. This had to be explained, down to the last detail, to both Mary and I, so we would both know exactly what to expect on the day. The more Ann went into this process the stranger it seemed to me, but I trusted her experience and listened to her instructions. Firstly, she asked me to decide if I wanted to bring anyone with me. I told her that I would love to bring my mum, to which she agreed, but when Mary and I actually met, Ann said, it would only be Ann, Mary and I in the room. If everybody felt comfortable, mum and Mary could meet at the end.

She also asked me if I wanted to walk into the room Mary was already in, or if I wanted to wait in a room and for Mary to walk in. Seems strange, I know, but she explained to me that it was important to organise every last detail to help things run smoothly on the day. When she asked if it was OK for Mary to give me a hug when we met and said that she would have a small table in the room between the two chairs where Mary and I would be sitting, in order to give us both our "personal space," I thought she was going too far. Then I realised that I had never met this woman before and it would be an emotional day, so I accepted that Ann knew best.

I decided I would feel more comfortable walking into a room Mary was already in. Ann told me that she would walk with me into the room, to meet Mary for the first time, and that she would stay for around fifteen minutes or so, until we were both comfortable. Then she would leave us to chat for two hours. She would intermittently come in and out to make sure we were both still OK, but if we wanted to take a picture together, we were not to do it until the end. Then she would call it a day because that would be enough for us both to deal with.

It would be an exciting day, but also difficult and draining, she said.

One of the last things Ann explained to me was the importance of not being late on the day, but also not to be early, as she wanted to arrange for Mary to be there fifteen minutes before me. She didn't want us meeting for the first time on the doorstep.

I hung up the phone from Ann that day and I couldn't allow myself to think about what was going to happen in just two days' time. I was afraid to. If I thought too much about it, I might lose my nerve. So, I did what a lot of twenty-year-old girls would have done, and went shopping. Impatient and impulsive, yet I run away when the going gets tough!

It was the first time I looked back at all the things over the last few years that I had started and then quit and, I decided, I wasn't going to talk myself out of this one – so I had to keep busy. I wanted to look my best on the day that I was going to meet my birth mother for the first time anyway, so I searched through shop after shop in an effort to find something I wanted to wear.

It didn't really matter, I suppose, but it helped me to take my mind off what was going to be one of the biggest steps of my life. Clothes bought, make up bought and hair done.

Now all I had to do was wait until Friday.

One more day until I saw Mary!

One more day until I met the person who gave me life!

One more day until I had the answers to all of my questions!

But would I be ready to hear them all?

Would they hurt me?

Or would I understand?

Would I do my usual and run away?

I didn't know. I hadn't a clue, when faced with the reality of the situation, how I was going to react. I had lay awake in bed so many nights throughout my life, dreaming about this day, wanting it to happen so much, but I don't think I had ever been so terrified.

I didn't sleep a wink the night before, with every question and scenario racing through my mind, and by 8am I still hadn't got anything any clearer in my head. I had simply decided *here goes nothing!*

Time to grow up, Aoife. I reminded myself. *Remember you wanted this.*

Chapter 10 – This is it!

ON the way in I went over everything Ann had told me, with my mum, and when that was done she tried to ease the nerves by chatting about day to day things.

"With all of this going on, I hope you haven't missed out on too much in college?"

"I explained everything to the college, Mum. They have been great and have been emailing me the lectures."

"Yes," she replied with a smile, but knowing me added, "But have you been looking at them?"

I couldn't help but giggle. "It will be fine, I met Brid for a few drinks last night and she filled me in on all that's going on."

"All that's going on, on the social side of things, knowing you! Just remember not to neglect your studies."

"Of course, Mum," I replied, just to keep her happy.

It was a warm September morning and the city centre was awash with people going about their day, enjoying the sunshine. In the distance a busker with a guitar was singing Robbie Williams' *Angels* and as I took in all the people around me I began to wonder where they were all going. *Did anyone else around me have an important day ahead too?* They certainly didn't look like they had a care in the world. I wished I felt the same. Thankfully though Mum, as ever, was amazing and doing a great job of keeping me calm and relaxed. As we walked through the city, following the same path to the adoption agency that my parents had taken all those years ago, to meet their children for the first time, I looked at her and marvelled at the wonderful role model she had always been.

Eventually we reached the big green door. I didn't knock at first. I took a minute, looked at my mum and just stared straight ahead at the golden arch around the top of the door, and the big brass handle. I couldn't help but wonder how many people's lives had been changed forever by lifting this handle, knocking on this door and walking under the arch. My birth mother had knocked on this door and walked through to the other side, but in doing so she lost the child she had carried for nine months. My parents, however, knocked twice on this big green door, walked through to the other side and gained two children as a result. This door changed people's lives.

For better or for worse – who knew what way it would go for me?

Eventually, and with all the courage I could muster, I took a step up and knocked on the green door. *What would I gain? What would I lose?* I really didn't know but I decided in those few minutes that it didn't matter who it was lifting up the heavy brass handle. Every single person who stepped up and walked through to the other side had something in common. Whether they were a birth mother or father looking for help giving a child for adoption, an adoptive parent filling out their first application forms or coming to collect their child for the first time or, like me, a child, lost and looking for answers about where they came from. Every one of us had the courage to come here and at the very least deserved an answer.

I looked at mum again who was watching me struggle – no words were needed but I felt her reassurance that no matter how this day went, everything was going to be OK. Finally I took one last deep breath, lifted the handle and heard the loud knock echo through the large empty hallway.

Ann came to the door with a look of both anticipation and excitement on her face. She was dressed up more than usual in a flowing flowery dress and was clutching her hands in front of her as she told me that Mary was waiting for me. She then led us into an office where my mum would wait.

Then it was my time to climb the stairs and with each step I took I could feel my heart pounding in my chest, almost in sync with my footsteps. As it turned out Ann was bringing me up to the very same room that, twenty years before, my mum had waited in for me to be placed in her arms for the first time. Ann pushed open the door and held it for me as I gingerly entered almost hiding behind her like a child.

And there she was. It had been two decades of wondering everything from what she looked like, to what she sounded like and now here she was in front of me. I was almost afraid to look at her. As soon as Mary saw me though, she stood up with tears in her eyes and we slowly walked towards each other before falling into each other's arms and crying for ourselves as we held each other tight.

It felt like neither of us spoke for such a long time but it wasn't an awkward silence, it was apt.

Eventually we stood back and even though the rush of emotions were nearly too much to handle, I couldn't take my eyes off her. We did look like each other. We were the same height, had the same hair colour and the same eyes. I had never met anyone who I could say I looked like before and I was stunned by it. For a long time we just stood there staring at each other before crying again for what felt like an eternity. I couldn't speak. I had lost all capacity to say anything at all. That I hadn't expected. I had played this day out a million times, had a million questions in my head and now it was real and I couldn't get one word out. I guess Ann knew things might start off that way so she bridged the gap.

"Aoife has been so nervous waiting outside, Mary, this really is such a huge step for you both."

And then I heard Mary speak for the first time. She sounded nothing like the voice I had imagined thousands of times in my head. She wasn't that lost little girl anymore, terrified to be pregnant. She was a beautiful, strong, warm and caring lady.

"I have been sitting in this room going crazy watching the door and staring at the picture you gave me with your letter. You are beautiful, I don't want to let you go," she said over my shoulder, while hugging me tighter than anyone ever had before.

"If I had known it was you looking for me I would have responded straight away," she managed to get out through her tears.

It wasn't long before I found my voice because her presence made me feel comfortable.

"I feel like this is a dream," I stammered. "I have been waiting so long for this day and now that you are here, after all this time, I don't know what to say or where to start."

"We can start anywhere you like," Mary said as she took my hand and led me to a chair.

She had a way of making me feel relaxed very quickly, so it wasn't long before we got going. We were only scratching the surface but after a short time we were talking like we had been long lost friends. It felt right straight away and we seemed to get each other. We even had the same mannerisms. After a while Ann could see that we were doing great and that we were comfortable with each other, so she left us alone to talk.

As soon as she left the room Mary started laughing and said: "I was so relieved when you walked into the room, by the way Ann had described you I didn't know what to expect."

I had a few pink extensions in my hair and my eyeliner was my best friend but I was no different to any other twenty-year-old at the time.

"I looked exactly like you at your age," she added and we both smiled.

It was so strange. I had never spoken to this person sitting across from me before, yet there was not one single awkward silence. Not one moment of not knowing what to say to each other after that initial few minutes, and at one point we even moved the little table out of the way so we could have our chairs right beside each other. I felt so comfortable and it was just right.

Every now and then Ann would pop her head in, which in all honesty just interrupted our conversation, but we would get right back into it when she left again. I told Mary all about my childhood, my parents and my brother. How adoption had affected me in a good way and a bad. It was easy to be honest with her and not hold back. We talked about my friends, school and college and she even repeated the same sentence mum had said earlier that day: "I hope you haven't been missing too much time in college with all this going on?"

I just smiled and replied, "maybe a little."

It is hard to fill in a twenty-year gap but we were doing a good job at getting started and getting to know a little bit more about each other. Mary told me about her life, her husband and her kids. She told me about her family, her job and how she reacted when she finally got that phone call from Ann. She genuinely had no idea I had been looking for her and was shocked when she suddenly put the meaning of the letters together.

Then the conversation came around to the time I was adopted. It was hard listening to Mary tell me about it from her point of view. I could hear the pain still in her voice as she talked about how much she questioned her decision and how hard it was. She had kept that pain and guilt with her all that time and even when she was in labour with her daughter, who was then 6, she said she relived the experience all over again but just cried and cried, keeping all those emotions bottled up inside, not able to share them with anyone.

I wished I could have told her before that moment that I was OK. Maybe then, things would have been a little bit easier for her. After all, she must have felt so alone carrying such a big secret by herself for so long.

*

You are probably wondering why I haven't written about my birth father until now. It was pretty simple to me at the time with the information the adoption agency had given us when I was first adopted. It said that when Mary had told my birth father that she was pregnant with me, he wasn't that interested or supportive to her and didn't want to really be involved in any way, leaving Mary alone. I grew up with an amazing dad who would have gone to the ends of the earth to have children, so would I want to get to know, or have anything to do with, a man who would not even stand up to his responsibilities? He ran away (as far as I was concerned) and so I thought he was a coward and when the conversation came around to him, I could tell it was still very difficult for Mary to speak about – and then I realised why.

"I was young and scared and after Ann had recently read my notes back to me, I realised it painted a very different picture of John – one that I would not have wanted. He didn't run away, maybe he would have, he was no saint, but he didn't run away. He wasn't given the chance. He had never known, and still doesn't know about you, Aoife!"

For the first time that day I was shocked. Mary and my birth father had the same big group of friends. When she was at a friend's wedding and was planning to tell him she was pregnant he had been there with a different girl when she arrived so she felt like she couldn't tell him and that was obviously the end of the relationship. Mary didn't see him again after that.

I sat there listening to her speak about John, my birth father, with so much pain still in her eyes and so much regret that I couldn't feel anything but pity for her. I knew it must have been so difficult for her at the time, as well as devastating to be betrayed like that, so I wasn't mad but I was knocked for six for the first time that day. I just found it hard to get the thought clear in my head that I had dismissed this man my whole life, for something he didn't do. I had labelled him a coward when I had no idea if that was true or not. He didn't run away, because he never knew. I respected Mary so much for having the courage to tell me all of this now and we chatted about it for a little while, but not in any great depth. We had so much else to talk about too!

Later Mary went on to tell me that she had informed Ann, and given her any details she had, about John and where he was living twenty years ago, in case I ever felt I wanted to find him. She also said she would support me.

We continued on jumping from one conversation to the next. There was so much we wanted to know about each other. Mary told me that her two kids couldn't wait to meet me and the next time we met, she would love me to meet her husband. One two-hour period in my life and I had so many answers to questions that had haunted me for years.

It was hard to comprehend how amazing that feeling was. Not only did I have so many answers, all the fear was now gone too. No more *what if she won't meet me? What if I will never know? What if she doesn't like me?* It was all out in the open and it was all going so well. All too soon though, once again, Ann popped her head around the door. I didn't want this day to end. It had been amazing. So much more than I had ever dreamed of, but the system was there for a reason and she told us we could come back to that room – which, I realised, was full of joy for some and heartache for others – and meet again soon.

Ann then looked at Mary and asked, "Would you like to meet Aoife's mum? She is waiting in the room downstairs and I know she would love to meet you, just for a few minutes before you leave?"

Mary replied with a smile, looking at me for approval, and answered immediately, "I would love to meet her."

Ann nodded and quickly left the room again to go and get mum, leaving

Mary and I alone one last time. "God, I think I am more nervous to meet your mum than I was to meet you," she joked.

I laughed and answered, "I don't blame you! Only joking, she is amazing and I bet she is nervous too."

I stood back as mum slowly opened the heavy door and entered the room. I wanted to give them their moment and it was amazing to see. For just a few moments they looked into each other's eyes and a thousand messages were passed without ever saying a thing. Then they moved towards each other like tentatively and gave each other a hug that said *thank you* to my mum for looking after the daughter that she had lost and *thank you* to Mary for giving my mum the daughter she might never have had.

Then they spoke. My mum first, saying, "You have been the subject of many conversations in our house over the years Mary. It is so lovely to finally have the opportunity to meet you. I have thought about you a lot throughout the years and I hope things haven't been too hard?"

With tears in her eyes Mary replied, "It has been such an emotional time since I realised that Aoife had been trying to contact me. I had no clue what those letters meant so this is all so new for me, but as soon as I knew I couldn't wait any longer. I just had to meet her. It helps me so much to finally know that she went to such a loving family. I have never stopped thinking about her, not once."

I stood in the background just watching, watching my birth mother and my mum have this special moment, standing, facing each other, holding hands and bonding over the one thing they had in common – me. Mary then hugged mum again and whispered something in her ear. I never did know what she said but it brought a tear to mum's eye and she turned to me and said, "You really do have a look of each other, how lovely."

I always knew what an amazing lady mum was and this was just another one of those times that brought it home for me.

Ann was hovering in the background and again stepped in saying, "I think it is time to go, what a nice way to end things for the day."

Mary and I then got a picture taken together, with mascara running down both our faces. Saying goodbye was harder than I ever imagined, harder than when we said hello. I was so preoccupied with how I was going to react when I met Mary that I never stopped to think about how I would feel saying goodbye.

I think it was the uncertainty of it because Ann had told us that we weren't allowed to tell each other where we lived yet, or swap telephone numbers, so I didn't know what was going to happen next. I did, however, leave without a doubt in my mind that this day was as special to Mary, as it was to me. I had so many of the answers I had needed for so long, but now, typically, I wanted to know more! I wanted to know all about her and her life. It wasn't enough for me anymore to just scratch the surface. I wanted to know the good things, the bad; even the things that I knew would be hard to hear. I wanted to know more about when I was adopted, and about my birth father. I hadn't given him much thought over the years but now that I knew my impression of him had been based on wrong information I wanted to know! He was, for the first time ever, creeping into my mind more and more and the impatient side of me was beginning to take over – but Mary felt the exact same. We were more alike than I ever thought possible!

I went home that day and phoned Amy, Clare and Katherine and asked them to come over. They were dying to hear how my day had gone. When I had come out of the adoption agency I had messages of support from them all and as we all sat around my kitchen table drinking tea and munching on biscuits I gave them a minute-by-minute account of the day I met my birth mother for the first time. I think they were as excited as I was that it had gone so well. It was still only sinking in for me and I could not wait to meet Mary again. You would think after twenty years of not knowing anything that I would be satisfied at least for a little while, finding out as much as I did in one day, but no! All I could think about was meeting her again.

Just a few days passed when my phone rang and the now familiar sight of the agency's number flashed up on the screen. Ann wanted to know how I was feeling about the big day and what I thought of Mary. I told her how delighted I was with how it all went and she told me she had been speaking to Mary and that she felt exactly the same. She would love to arrange another meeting at the adoption agency so I could meet her husband.
I was surprised Ann was telling me this so soon. It seemed like a dream come true and it was very difficult not to get carried away. I knew Mary and I had got on like a house on fire that first day, but I did have a lot more time to get used to the whole idea of us reuniting. For Mary to be as eager as me wasn't something I had expected and it was hard at times to remember to keep my feet on the ground, but it was vital that I did.

Chapter 11 – It was meant to be

THE day I went into the city to meet Mary and her husband for the first time, I felt comfortable enough to go in by myself. This time the nerves were replaced with excitement and when I heard the loud knock from the door echo through the hallway, I smiled to myself – remembering how it had taken all of my courage to even knock on that door just a few days previously. Again I climbed the staircase to the top and into the big bright room with all the windows. Again Mary was waiting for me, except this time her husband Mick was with her and they both stood up to greet me before I gave them both a hug. Ann only stayed with us a minute or two this time, as it was plain to see how comfortable we were with each other.

Mick was lovely. Just a few weeks before he didn't even known that I existed, so for him to be as relaxed and friendly as he was really meant the world to me. It can be difficult for any couple to talk about their past before they met each other, so this was a whole other level for him and it was hard, I'm sure – but Mick showed an unbelievable strength of character and it seemed to come easy for him. He is a true gentleman.

We spoke about so much that day. Again, jumping from one conversation to the next, but this time it was a lot more indepth. They told me about their two children and how excited *they* were with everything that was happening. I told them about the day I found out where they lived, seeing Mary and their son in the driveway, and we all had a laugh about it. They told me how amazing their whole family had been when they told them about me.

As soon as Mary had broken the news one of her brothers disappeared out of the house only to come back a few minutes later with a bottle of champagne – she had thought he might be angry! It all felt too good to be true. Once again the conversation turned to the time I was adopted. Mary had told me that she had requested her notes from twenty years ago as she was so traumatised at the time that she couldn't remember a lot of what happened – self-preservation forced her to block it out. I couldn't imagine what she had been through. I asked her more about my birth father and she told me more about him and his personality. She told me that he was from the west of Ireland and he sounded like he had been the life and soul of the party. Mary wanted me to know that he wasn't a bad guy, just a free spirit.

Ann, popping her head into the room, halted the conversation and as

Mary chatted with her, Mick asked me what I had been doing that summer. I told him about my holidays and that because the World Cup had been on that year, my friends and I had spent a lot of that time watching the matches in our local pub, The Orchard. Suddenly, with a huge smile on his face, Mick said "that's unbelievable!" As it turned out The Orchard was one of their local pubs and they had spent a lot of the World Cup matches in The Orchard too, with Mary's brother. Another one of my questions answered. *Had I ever walked past Mary on the street?* Not only was that more than likely, I had been in the same pub as her, at the same time, watching the same big screen all through the summer before I met her. I couldn't get that thought out of my head. What a small world, and to think I might not ever have known.

Ann then told us that she would give us another fifteen minutes but then we needed to finish up. Mary and I had spent those precious four hours together talking and talking about as much as we could fit in at this stage, but at the end of both meetings, neither of us felt like we were ready to leave. It was getting frustrating – having somebody else control your time with that precious person – but the structure was in place in case we hadn't got on! We had clicked though. More than I had ever imagined we would and we knew that Ann was going to offer us another two hour meeting for the following week, but it didn't seem enough anymore – for either of us. It still would, even then, only have been six hours we got to spend with each other after a lost twenty years. I knew Mary had been thinking the same as I was, just by looking at her face when Ann came in to tell us our time was nearly up and as soon as the door creaked closed again she looked at me with a cheeky grin and asked, "I know Ann will kill me for suggesting this but how would you feel if we were to swap details now and meet on our own terms next time? I know the kids would love to meet you and maybe you would like to come over to our house?"

I loved the idea that we were both on the same page, we both felt the same way and knew we were ready to take the next step. The only thing we were anxious about was how Ann would react to us moving away from the normal scheduling of these things, but we weren't like other people, we had connected and it felt right.

"Quickly let's do it before Ann comes back in and tells us it is a bad idea" I said feeling like a schoolgirl about to do something she knew she shouldn't.

As grateful as we both were to Ann for helping us to find each other, we were ready to fly solo, so I gave my phone number to Mary and she put it in her phone. I then took out my phone in order for Mary to give me her number and I started to enter it into my phone, but I was left feeling confused as I showed Mary the message that flashed up on my screen.

"Look what my phone says."

Mary read out loud as she looked at it. "Contact already exists? Well that doesn't make any sense, you must have a contact in there with a similar number to mine?" And we both laughed it off.

"Could you imagine?" I said, while deleting the number and starting over.

As soon as I had entered the last digit into my phone and pressed save, yet again, though, the same message flashed up on my screen informing me that the number already existed and was assigned to another contact. Feeling really confused I again showed Mary my phone and asked her to confirm I had entered the correct number. This just didn't make any sense to me.

She looked at it carefully with amazement. "That is my number, I don't understand." I was lost for words. *How could I possibly already have my birth mother's phone number?* Then I noticed the contact name beside the number it was already assigned to. Clare! My best friend Clare's name was assigned to Mary's number. There was so much going on at first that I couldn't figure out how this could be, but then I realised that it wasn't displaying Clare's current phone number, but her old one. I have known, and been best friends with Clare for as long as I can remember and when we were kids, Clare's family moved away for a couple of years. When they moved back to Dublin their old number was changed and I had put her new number in my phone as *Clare house new*. I never even thought about deleting her old number, which I had saved as *Clare home*. Every time I got a new phone over the years, I had just transferred over my old contacts and I somehow never even noticed I had still got it in there.

In Ireland, the way that the phone system worked, was that if a number had been changed and out of use for a certain amount of time, that number was then transferred and given to a new phone customer. In or around the same timeframe, Mary had returned to Ireland after working abroad and had bought a house with her husband. When they went to the phone company to set up their own private landline, they had been given Clare's old phone number. I couldn't get my head around it!

"I am sure I have dialled that number more than once by mistake since Clare changed it.

"There were so many coincidences," said Mary.

"We live so close to each other, we know our paths crossed before, at least once, during the World Cup and now this. Do you think somebody might be trying to tell us something here?" We all smiled.

"All of the years I spent searching for you," I said. "I was searching for answers that, since the beginning, were on my doorstep…and even as I sat in that registers' office, while I searched through pages of entries, it was for a number I had in my hand all along."

We were all incredulous.

"So close, but yet so far," Mary whispered.

I don't know why, but I took comfort from knowing that for eight years I had a connection to Mary, despite not knowing it. Mary on the other hand found it harder to deal with the missed opportunities to make things right. Of all the numbers in the entire world, she was given my best friend's one. Was this coincidence or fate? We would never know.

Our moment of amazement was soon interrupted by the door squeaking open again, and Ann's friendly face popping in to ask how we were getting on and we immediately told her that we had swapped contact information. Her smile quickly turned to a look of concern as she told us that she wasn't sure it was a good idea yet and asked would we not just agree to at least one more meeting, controlled by the adoption agency, before we took such a big step. In my head I was laughing telling myself, *I'm not going to forget that number now!*

We were expecting this response from Ann, because we knew that she wanted us both to follow the programme set out by the adoption agency, to the end, but we were both, at this stage, really frustrated by that very process. We understood why it all had to be in place but we felt that, for us, it was right to find our own way now.

We were both already so comfortable in each other's company and we wanted the decision of when we met, and for how long, to be in our own hands. We were ready to take the next step, so we respectfully thanked Ann for all of her support and advice and reassured her that this was what was right for both of us.

She respected our wishes but advised us to take things slowly and said that she was only ever at the other end of the phone if either of us needed her. We then said our goodbyes to Ann and to each other. There were no tears this time, just excitement about the next step of our journey and what the future held. For one last time I walked back through the big green door but this time I stopped as I reached the street and glanced back over my shoulder at it. With one big wave of emotion, I swallowed the lump in my throat as I thought about how walking through that very door had changed my life forever.

*

I was on top of the world and went home that day and got ready for a night out with my girls. No matter what was going on I couldn't miss my weekly Friday get together for a few drinks and a dance. I was turning into a bit of a party girl, which mum hated, as she could never get me up out of bed anymore!

Clare, Katherine and Amy never let one of my meetings with Mary pass without calling or texting me messages of support. They were always as excited as me and over a few cocktails that night I filled them in on my latest meeting with her. Clare was in shock when I told her about what had happened when we swapped phone numbers and kept saying, "Out of all the possible combination of numbers to choose from, Mary got mine!"

I believed more than ever that we were always supposed to meet. Our paths must have been meant to cross. From living so close to each other, to being in the same pub at the same time, and now this phone number thing.

I felt proud of myself for following things through with Mary. It gave me confidence, and a belief that I was growing up – because I had seen this through, despite being constantly tempted to run away.

Over the previous weeks I had been so busy with college and meeting Mary, that men and relationships hadn't entered my head; but that night I met Adam, who seemed like a nice guy, who was interested in me and so with my new-found confidence I thought I would give us a try. The girls, Adam and I had a great night and when it was time to leave he asked for my number.

Why not? I had answered.

Chapter 12 – So many hugs

THE next day, when I was home nursing a hangover from my night out with the girls, I got a text from Mary. She was inviting me over to her house the following day to meet her kids and family. I couldn't stop thinking about how brave she was. For someone to have kept such a huge secret to herself for twenty years, and gone through so much pain and suffering all alone, in just a few short weeks she had told her whole family and was welcoming me to meet them. I couldn't wait for Sunday to arrive, but I was terrified too.

It was a lot of people to meet all at once and they were all going to be there to meet me! I never imagined in my wildest dreams that I would ever have a day like this, but as happy as I was, I did feel a lot of pressure. Silly little things kept popping into my head like, *what if they don't like me? What if I don't know what to say?* I was so nervous.

I eventually decided that all I could do was be myself and remind myself that I had got on so well with Mary and Mick, so there was no reason why it should be any different with the rest of the family.

Before Sunday came I chickened out a little bit and asked Katherine if she would come with me for support, and she was happy to. As we made our way to Mary's, we took a slight detour to the McDonald's drive thru, for chips and a coffee and as we sat in the car, munching away, we both realised we were as nervous as each other.

"God, Aoife, I don't know how you did this by yourself the first day. I am so nervous to meet her and she isn't even anything to me!" said Katherine. "I just feel like she has been part of my life for ages too, because of the way you speak about her."

"I know," I replied. "But I still don't want to leave this car park. As much as I want to see her I am so scared every time – but I am proud of myself that I haven't run away yet and I don't intend to now either."

"Well, not *yet*," Katherine joked. "We all know what you're like."

Laughing in agreement and trying to take a sip of my coffee at the same time I ended up spilling the hot drink all down my trousers and the seat.

"I can't believe I just did that!" I shrieked. "That is so typical of me, but I haven't time to go home and get changed without being late."

Katherine, still laughing at me, replied, "Well at least now they will get to meet the real you... clumsy and smelling of coffee."

I couldn't help but join in her laughter as I started the engine of the car and we eventually headed for Mary's. The light-hearted conversation soon turned to tension, the closer I got to her house, and when we reached the estate my heart was nearly pounding out of my chest – just like it was the last time I drove there. Katherine was looking around in amazement.

"I can't believe all of this time she has been this close!"

"I know, it's crazy."

We drove around the corner and towards her house at the back. There were children playing on the green close to her home and I couldn't help but wonder if any of those little kids were my brother and sister.

I parked the car outside Mary's house, took a few deep breaths and Katherine and I then got out.

"I am sure we are going to make a great impression, smelling of chips and coffee, I still can't believe you did that," Katherine joked, trying to ease the tension.

I was more nervous this time than I was the first time I ever met Mary and I was so grateful to have Katherine with me. I needed the support. She was always there in my times of need, to help me through – even if it was just to slag me off or make me smile.

Standing on the doorstep waiting for Mary to open the door Katherine saw the look on my face and took my hand.

"Here goes nothing," she said with a smile.

She couldn't believe it when Mary opened the door and was visibly shocked at how much we looked like each other. Mary, who was nervous too, immediately gave me a big hug and led us into the kitchen, which was filled with people and smelled of freshly baked cookies. I felt so overwhelmed. I didn't know where to look or who was who – or even who to say hello to first! Then a friendly-looking older lady caught my eye as she sat at the end of the long kitchen table and smiled up at me. Now I knew where to start. I may not have known who was who yet, in relation to the other people that filled the room, but I knew this smiling, petite lady was Mary's mother, my grandmother. I headed straight for her and as I got closer her warm smile melted all my nervous tension away.

She stood up to greet me and gave me a hug.

"It is so wonderful to meet you, Aoife, it has been a huge shock to find out about you, but a really great one."

I smiled at her, not knowing what to say, and then she continued, "Am I 'Gran' or would you like to call me by my name?"

Without hesitation I smiled at my grandmother for the first time and replied, "You're Gran."

They were my first words, to her and in front of this room full of strangers and I could not have thought of any better way to start out.

In probably one of the scariest rooms I have ever walked into, one warm welcome, one smile from my grandmother after I met her for the first time, and I felt at home. I turned to the other people then and every last one of them had the same welcoming look on their face. One by one I met everyone – the aunts, uncles, cousins and, of course, my beautiful little brother and sister. I felt like I had won the lottery.

Everything I had ever dreamed of, or ever wanted, was coming true and in a much bigger way than I ever even thought possible. This whole new relationship we were at the beginning of was something I never even considered a possibility.

Katherine and I stayed in Mary's that day for hours and we were made to feel so welcome. All the fear had disappeared within five minutes of walking through the front door and it was surprisingly easy to talk to everyone. They were all so interested in hearing all about me. Mary and I were both really enjoying the relaxed atmosphere that came from meeting on our own terms and not having anyone else control our time together too. I enjoyed every second, especially getting to know my little brother and sister who showed me their rooms and toys, and we really bonded. When it was time to leave, my cheeks hurt from smiling and laughing so much and my eyes looked tired because there were a few tears of joy also. I was emotionally drained, but elated at the same time. Every last one of my uncles and aunts and cousins gave me a hug and welcomed me to the family, but eventually, again we said our goodbyes.

On the way home in the car neither of us had the energy to talk much and I couldn't help but think quietly to myself, *maybe I am changing, maybe I'm growing up! After all I have jumped in, yet again, to an overwhelming situation, and faced it. I haven't run away, and it hasn't been easy, but I'm doing it. Yeah, I need the support of mum and my friends, but I'm still doing it.*

Katherine interrupted my train of thought by asking, "You look smug, what are you smiling about?"

"I just had a great day, thanks for coming hun," I replied simply.

"You're welcome, you better go home and get ready, aren't you meeting Adam tonight?"

"Yes," I replied with a smile. "We are meeting for a drink and I've already picked out my outfit, but before you head off can you do my nails?"

"Of course," she laughed and I smiled my thanks.

*

We had many more days like the first one in the following few weeks and

Mary and I got to know each other really well. I was invited over to Sunday dinners and birthday parties. Everything was working out so well – and then the strangest thing happened. I began to run into her, randomly, everywhere! In a shopping centre, at traffic lights on my way to a night out with my girls in a taxi… Everywhere!

I even began to run into her brother in the pub a few times. I couldn't help but wonder, again, was it coincidence or fate? And how many times had we been in the same place at the same time and looked each other in the eye without knowing who the other was. I had never, ever, had such a feeling of peace. I was so settled, and happier then I could ever remember. I was more confident than ever before too, but life has a habit of surprising you and turning everything on its head right when you're on top of the world…

*

Things were beginning to seem normal again. There was no more waiting for the phone to ring. No more nerve-racking meetings. The hype and excitement of meeting Mary and her family had died down and I was simply enjoying getting to know her. Having the answers to so many of the questions that had been racing through my mind for twenty years meant the world to me and I was happy and relaxed. Happy with the relationship Mary and I were building and happy with all of the support I had got, and continued to get, from mum and dad. I couldn't have done any of this without them and because of them I was happy. I was settled. Life was great.

Adam had flaked on a couple of dates but he seemed to have a good excuse and always made up for it after. The old me would have always over analysed things, but I was stronger now and taking things in my stride so I decided I wasn't going to ruin this for myself. I was going to go with the flow and allow myself to be happy for once. After all he was still a nice guy.

Admittedly I was still a little bit uneasy about finding out that Mary had never told my birth father about me. Knowing there was a man out there somewhere that had never even known he had a child, felt wrong. He had never been given the chance to step up to the plate and do the right thing and I felt guilty for wrongly judging him for so long.

Don't get me wrong; I never blamed Mary for any of the decisions she had made, she was only doing what she felt was right for her at the time and besides, if Mary hadn't made the decisions she did all those years ago, I wouldn't have the amazing parents that I have now and I wouldn't be the person I am. But, still, thoughts of John, and the missed opportunities he'd had, were never far from my mind. I felt like most of the puzzle pieces in my

82

Mum and Dad's wedding day

Mum and Dad on holidays

My first day in my new home

Mum and Carl

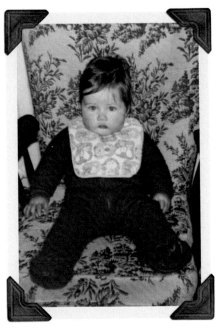

My big brother

Always together

Good times

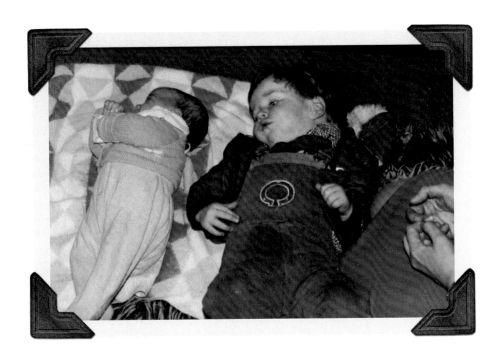

Going to see Mum in hospital

Holiday in Spain after Mum's Cancer treatment

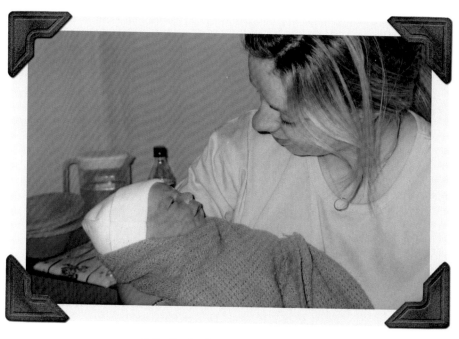

My little boy is just born

Jack arriving home

Jack and Grandad

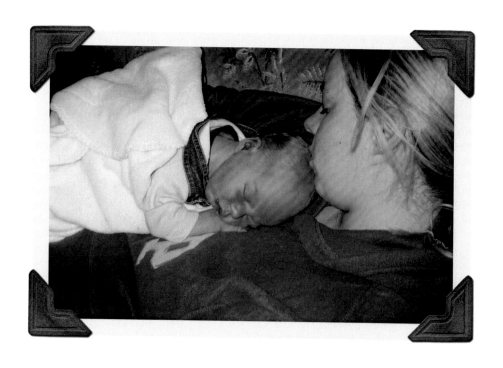

Getting used to being a Mummy

Have I got ice cream on my face?

Me and my girls

Me and my girls

Me and Dan

Me and Dan

Enjoying a day off

Carl and I – Still best friends

Our beautiful children

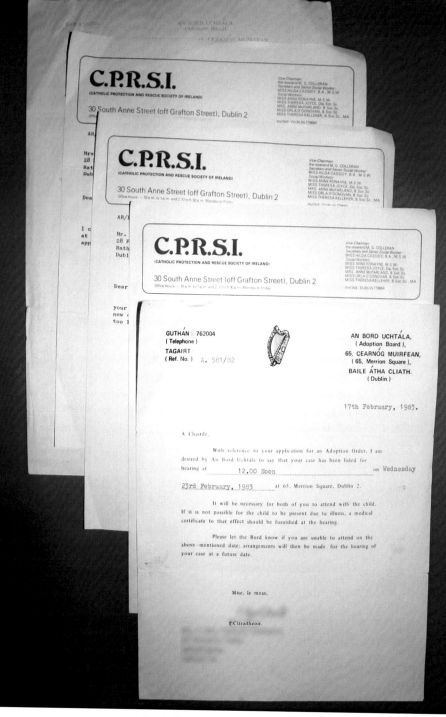

My Adoption Paperwork

life, that had been missing for so long, were finally fitting into place – except this one…

Then something happened that threw everything up in the air again and my thoughts and concerns went out the window, only to be replaced with sheer panic.

My period was late!

Chapter 13 – Two little blue lines

MARY was 24 and alone when she fell pregnant with me and she couldn't cope. I was 20, I wasn't alone but I couldn't ignore the annoying feeling that Adam would let me down.

This couldn't be happening to me.

I was young and naive and I hadn't thought Adam was using me but in hindsight, it was obvious that he was. He was young too, just a couple of years older than me, and I guess I knew that we wouldn't end up in a serious relationship – not that a serious relationship was really on my radar either. One thing was for sure though, my period was never late and I think on some level I knew I had to be pregnant. Still though, for a few days I convinced myself that I was just being paranoid. *I couldn't possibly be pregnant. History couldn't really be repeating itself like this, right at this moment in time, when I had just met Mary. Could it?*

By the fifth day I couldn't ignore it anymore. There was a voice in my head screaming at me to just find out and I couldn't ignore it any longer. Time to be brave again! I phoned my friend Gill, who had, just three weeks before, found out that she was unexpectedly pregnant by her long-term boyfriend. I knew she would help me. I couldn't face telling Adam, who had already come up with an excuse not to go on an arranged night out with my friends and me, so if I had news for him I needed it to be face to face.

Gill came with me to buy the pregnancy test. To say I was scared would have been the understatement of the year. I was absolutely terrified.

When I finally built up the courage to take it (about an hour later) it was the longest three minutes of my life.

Watching that little window and waiting to see one blue line or two, my life, and how it would change, was flashing before my eyes. And suddenly there it was – my answer as clear as day. I was pregnant. I was alone and I was terrified and for a split second, as I stood there shaking with tears in my eyes, not knowing how to feel, I saw a true glimpse of what Mary must have felt all those years ago.

Huge questions started to flood my mind. *Why me? Why now? Can I do this? Am I strong enough? Who can I tell? How will I tell my parents? What will they say? How will I tell Adam? Will he be there or will he run?*

I found myself seeking refuge – alone in my car, but I eventually got myself together enough to go home. I couldn't even look my mum in the eye and I sat up that whole night alone, numb, just watching the little flashing clock on the DVD player. I had never felt so scared and I was panicking and crying. Nothing made any sense. *How would I get through the next few days let alone the next nine months?*

I phoned Katherine first thing the next morning and she came with me to the doctor to confirm the pregnancy. We sat in the waiting room, which smelt like antiseptic and was full of strangers, trying not to talk about the elephant in the corner. We looked at fashion magazines and celebrity gossip until, eventually, we heard my name being called from the reception desk. I looked at Katherine's face full of fear and I felt like my feet were stuck to the floor as I whispered, "If I don't go in, then all this can go away, it won't be real."

But she stood up and simply took my hand before saying, "This won't go away you need to be strong, but, Aoife, you're not on your own. I am here and we will get through this together."

That was all I needed – that and one more deep breath, before I put one foot in front of the other until I found myself standing in front of the doctor, still holding Katherine's hand. The doctor had squeezed me in for a last-minute appointment before lunch, after I told the secretary on the phone that it was an emergency, and he didn't look best pleased. I never noticed how scary he could look. He had always greeted me with a smile before, but not today. He was a tall broad man, standing over six feet tall, with a long beard – and his aftershave always made me sneeze.

"Now then," he said in a stern voice. "What is so important that it couldn't wait until after my lunch?"

All his tone did was make everything more frightening as he stared at me with a disapproving look over the rim of his glasses. My newly-found confidence had left me and I felt like a lost little girl again, afraid to respond. Katherine couldn't bear to watch me struggle so she decided to have confidence for me.

"Aoife thinks that she is pregnant," she said as she ushered me into the seat in front of him.

"I see," he replied.

"You have taken a pregnancy test I assume?"

Not yet able to find my voice I simply nodded my head as I wiped away the tears that were now flowing down my face and onto my top.

"And what do you want me to do?"

His response shocked me as I had thought the first thing you should do if you get a positive pregnancy test is to see a doctor.

"I thought you could confirm it for me," I answered in a timid voice.

"Very well," he responded. "But I hope you aren't expecting a different outcome. If you have taken a test that has been positive, then it is positive," he growled, as he handed me a jar for a sample.

After he pointed in the direction of the toilet I left as fast as I could to get away.

Waiting and watching the doctor carry out another pregnancy test in silence all I could think of was how I was going to get out of this office without totally falling apart. Once the test was complete he looked up from his desk and said, "Well as I have told you if one test says you are pregnant then you are pregnant."

He showed me the positive result and without a care for my reaction he continued, "Right, let's get this organised. What hospital do you want to attend to have your baby?"

As he registered the look of shock on my face he impatiently added, "These are things you should have thought about and I really can't understand why you are crying."

Even in 2003, when life in Ireland was supposed to be a different place from the one Mary had felt she would be judged and left alone in, I was facing the same prejudice from a doctor who was clearly of the opinion that I had made my bed so I should lie in it. As a twenty-year-old girl who was brought up to respect her elders, doctors and teachers, I was now being let down by a man who had a huge amount of respect in the community. I just didn't understand at the time how wrong his attitude towards me was.

I thought, if he believed that I was a stupid naive little girl who needed to just deal with it, then what hope would I have of getting any support from anyone else? The final straw was when he asked me if I had learned from my "stupid mistake," before telling me to go home and tell my parents. I couldn't get out of his office quick enough.

This man had been my doctor for as long as I could remember, but I knew I would never walk through those doors again. He made me feel dirty and more scared than ever to tell anyone else. If I could say anything to any young girl now, who finds herself in a similar situation with a similarly ignorant reaction, it's this – Although we live in a world where unfortunately people like that do exist, never let anyone else judge you, or make you feel like you don't deserve support. No matter what your situation is, or how alone you feel, there is support out there and you will get through it. Do not let anyone else's old-fashioned ignorant words drag you down, like I did.

Katherine

The day I found out Aoife was expecting – in fact the day Aoife found out – is as vivid in my memory as if it were yesterday.

The doorbell rang, mam answered, and I could hear Aoife's familiar footsteps running up to my room. She burst through the door closing it behind her – clearly in some kind of panic.

I remember saying "What's wrong?" as all sorts of bad things ran through my mind. She looked worried and then she told me she had done a test and it was positive.

My first reaction was "Oh no," but obviously I just wanted to make her feel better. I knew I needed to be calm for her so I suggested we make an appointment with her doctor and have it confirmed before she told anyone else.

We must have looked so young sitting in that waiting room, waiting for her to be called. Then she went in, as well as could be, but came out upset. The doctor had not dealt with the situation in the most sensitive of ways. His old-fashioned attitude towards this young single mother only further amplified our concerns about what people would think.

Aoife had many ups and downs during her pregnancy as a young girl feeling frightened and unsure of the future. A few months later, to my disbelief, I found myself in the same situation and Aoife was there for me in the same way as I was for her. It was a little different for me in that I was in a relationship but that didn't make it any less scary – just maybe a little easier to face the dreaded public opinion.

We both got through our pregnancies and went on to have sons who are only six months apart in age – two great children.

Looking back at us sitting in that doctor's waiting room, if only we had known that our fear of how we would be judged by our decisions was the very least of our worries. It was the massive task of bringing two little boys up that should have been our cause for concern.

I came out of the doctors that day feeling like I had gone through six rounds in a boxing ring. How could I tell my parents? I just wasn't strong enough to deal with anyone else judging me, and so I convinced myself that it was a good idea to not tell anyone else because I was so emotional and weak. I didn't feel strong enough to deal with my own emotions let alone anyone else's. I never anticipated, however, how difficult it would be to act as if everything was OK. I barely got through breakfast in the same room as my parents. The guilt was destroying me and I felt like I couldn't even take a breath until I heard the front door close the following morning and they had both gone off to work. I spent the rest of the morning trying to convince myself that I could do it, *don't tell anyone, be strong.* I thought I was OK and I had it clear in my head that I was going to keep this to myself – until I heard my mum's key in the door later that day. She walked through the hall and into the kitchen where I was. I had been baking cupcakes, trying to keep my mind busy. Mum and I always loved to make cupcakes together and I would always get the mixture out of the bowl once we were finished.

"Hi, love. Lovely, you have made cupcakes, just what I need! They will go lovely with a cup of tea."

She didn't get a chance to take her coat off, or sit down. She hadn't even pushed down the button on the kettle, when I lost all control over what I was doing or saying and before I knew what I had done, I blurted out "I'm pregnant!"

She stood there in front me as I burst into tears. I hadn't even imagined what her reaction would be; I just knew I was scared. I had built it up so much in my head. But at that exact moment, all conscious thought left me and I was just a blubbering mess standing in my mum's kitchen. She remained where she was for a minute, obviously in shock, and then simply, as if it were the most natural thing in the world, gave me a hug and said she would pop the kettle on to make me a sweet cup of tea for the shock. She then pulled out a chair for me to sit down and handed me the bowl and a spoon with the left over cupcake mixture.

Most of that afternoon mum just listened. She didn't ask questions, she just made sure that I knew I wasn't alone and she would always be there. I don't know why I expected anything else. Mum had always been my rock, but I will especially never forget the love and support she showed me that day. I wouldn't have got through any of it without her.

Sometimes the closer you are to somebody the harder it is to tell them something you think will let them down. For this reason, I couldn't face my dad. I didn't even tell this to my mum, yet somehow she knew and asked me if I wanted her to tell him, to which I said yes. Shaking, I decided I wanted to be away from the house until she did, and a couple of hours later I got a call. It was dad and he just said, "Please come home."

I was so nervous. I don't know why, because anyone who knows my dad knows how much of a gentle soul he is, but I just didn't want to let him down. I pulled up at the house and he opened the front door when he saw my car, then stood, arms open wide, without need for a single word.

I ran into that hug, so relieved that everything was OK, and I knew then that whatever happened, so long as I had my parents, it would be. I couldn't imagine how Mary got through that first day, let alone nine months, without that reassuring hug – that loving support.

That night was the hardest part of that whole day for me because I went into my mum's room for a chat and for the first time in my whole life I saw her cry. Mum was always the shoulder for everyone in our family, the strong one, yet there she was, weak and vulnerable. I honestly thought my heart would break. Not for me but for her. I know she was wondering how I would cope and even though it must have brought up some painful memories of the difficulties she had conceiving, I knew her tears were for me, and not for herself. I sat on the side of her bed and tried to comfort her and act strong, but even in her weakest moments she still ended up being the one supporting me.

"I don't mean to worry you Mum, please don't cry."

Wiping away her tears with her sleeve she looked at me then and said, "Aoife, it is just a shock, but at the end of the day you're OK. It is a new life and we will all get through this one way or another, together. I don't want you to worry about how we are doing, we will all get used to this. I want you to concentrate on getting everything straight in your head. You need to be strong, we all do, but no matter what, we are all going to love this baby so much. It's just a shock right now, that's all."

Then tears started again, but this time it was me, not mum, as she asked me the question I had been dreading.

"I am assuming the father is that guy, Adam, you were seeing? But I haven't heard you mention him in a while."

She had never even met Adam and I hadn't found the courage to tell him at that stage so I couldn't even reassure her by telling her that he knew and would be there for me. We hadn't spoken in a few days. I'd sent him a text that morning but I hadn't had a reply.

"Mum, I am so scared to tell him. Honestly, I could be doing all of this by myself. I have no clue how he is going to react. I don't even know how I am going to have the courage to tell him."

And there it was, just as I said those words out loud, the fear of rejection all over again. The last time I felt that fear was when I thought Mary wasn't responding to my letters, but still this felt different. I think in my heart I knew the possibility of rejection was pretty much a certainty. Even then when it was all sinking in, mum didn't ask me any more questions about him. I think it was because she knew I wasn't strong enough to answer them. She just listened for a while and eventually looked me straight in the eye and concluded, "Whether Adam is going to be there or not, don't ever think you will be alone."

We sat in silence for another while after that, just staring at the telly but not really watching it and eventually lay on mum's bed, both of us totally drained from the day's events.

Mum

It was a Tuesday afternoon in December and I had just come in from my voluntary work as counsellor with a crisis pregnancy agency. I was wearing my green wax raincoat and I came home to be greeted by Aoife, baking in the kitchen. "I have something to tell you, I'm pregnant," she suddenly blurted out and I stood there rooted to the spot. I couldn't speak, I couldn't even hug her at first, I was numb. Still wearing my coat I slumped into the chair and my mind began to race. We had just celebrated our 25th wedding anniversary with a wonderful party and as I sat looking at the photographs, some weeks later, I realised there had been five of us in the picture. A lot had happened in the previous few months between the anniversary and Aoife making contact with Mary. Then suddenly a thought hit me "Good God it could be twins!" Mary was a twin and I thought, whatever about coping with one, how could we cope with two? The next thought I had going through my mind was "How is Mac going to react to this?" I offered to tell him. When he came home I decided I would wait and let him enjoy his dinner, but just as he finished the last bite I began to speak "There is no easy way to tell you this, Aoife is pregnant." He gulped and gasped and sat back in his chair and as he sat there in silence for a moment I thought of Mary. Mary had been in the same boat twenty years previously – it might help Aoife to talk to her.

After that it was a case of making maternity appointments with the hospital and we all tried to be there for her as much as we could. Aoife had a scare one Saturday morning where we needed to rush her to the hospital. Thank God the baby was fine, I think that was the day that we realised we were all coming to terms with the idea and we were all so relieved that the baby was OK. It was that day I thought about telling people. My sister, who sadly has dementia now, was the first person I told. We were at a concert together and during the interval I told her. I still wasn't used to saying it out loud. I phoned my other two sisters that night and told them too and they were all so positive and supportive. Telling my friends was different, I didn't feel like I could tell them on the phone for some reason, I wanted to be face to face with them when I told them. I suppose I felt it was too important to relay on the phone and I didn't want Aoife hearing and thinking I was speaking about her either. At the end of the day her feelings were so important and as much as I could get support from my friends and my brother and sisters I needed to give my support to her – that was my priority.

*

From the second those two little blue lines changed my life, I was terrified, but there was one thing I was sure of, this was my baby and scared or not, I was going to keep him or her. I think for me, because I am adopted, it was a question I had asked myself many times over the years. *Could I give a child up for adoption?* The answer was always no. I understood why people, including Mary, felt like that was the best option for them and I do think it took a lot of bravery for Mary to make that decision and acknowledge that at that point in her life she couldn't give a baby everything that a baby needs. However, being an adopted child, it wasn't the right decision for me. I knew from the second I saw those two blue lines, it was going to be my baby and that, scared or not, I was going to get through it and, alone or not, I was going to love this baby more than anything. I just had to get over the shock first. I had the support of two loving parents and they wanted me to believe that I could get through anything, so I would.

For the next couple of weeks, whenever I pulled my car into the driveway, my dad was there at the front door waiting for me with open arms, knowing that I would be coming home in tears. It was just so difficult to take it all in and they knew that Adam had not responded to my texts to meet up.

To comprehend the extent in which my life would change forever was so overwhelming and I was beginning to feel more and more alone as Adam's silence made it clear he was no longer interested in me.

Mary would be another hurdle. I didn't know how I was going to face her and tell her that history was repeating itself, but I did know that she would be the one person in my life that would truly understand how I was feeling and how terrified I was – if I could just let her know. Only twenty years before, she had been in the exact same situation and, like her, fear had taken over and I hadn't yet told the father. I know I wasn't given the chance to tell him, but I still felt like a coward.

One day I was on my way over to babysit her kids, my brother and sister, and I was trying to talk myself into feeling strong enough to do it then, by reminding myself that her experiences would help me and that she would know how I was feeling, but the strength didn't last long. When I pulled up to Mary's house Mick was there, as was her mum.
They were always so welcoming and friendly towards me, but they were heading off with Mary to her graduation, from a course she had completed, so it was definitely not the time. I spent that day with the kids, which helped me keep my mind off everything. I loved spending time with them, but that night when they went to bed, I sat in Mary's kitchen, alone and drinking a cup of tea. Then all of a sudden it hit me again like a tonne of bricks. *If Mary couldn't do this with me, how could I ever get through it?* She seemed like such a strong, calm and collected person. I didn't feel strong. I felt like a lost child. I remember hearing their car pull up, just as I was trying to fix my makeup, and I began to panic.

She knew something was up the minute she walked in and I felt like I couldn't breathe, so I quickly made my excuses and got out of there as soon as I could. I really couldn't face her. It had only been a few months since she had relived the time when she was pregnant with me and how traumatic it was, I just felt like she would want something different for me and I simply couldn't tell her.

My car seemed to be the place that saw most of my tears for those few weeks.

Driving home that night, I couldn't control myself. I had never been so scared and confused. One minute I felt strong and collected and the next I was in tears again, not able to get one clear thought in my head. I felt so out of control.

That night I drove into my driveway and there was my dad, arms open and ready to help. He simply said, "Come into the kitchen and I'll make you a sweet cup of tea." Mum, from the next room, heard that I was upset again so she came in to join us and walking into the kitchen she said, "I will phone Mary and tell her so you don't have to feel the pressure of getting the words out, and then Mac can drive you back up to her house and go with you. She is the one person who knows what you are going through; I think she will be able to help."

There they were again. My parents, my rocks! I didn't even have to ask them, they just knew.

"Can you at least get changed first though?" I said to my dad smiling. "I don't think I can take any more of your socks with sandals, and don't forget to take off the bum bag too!"

"That's the daughter I know and love. I knew you were in there some-where!" He grinned.

We finished our tea then and headed back over to Mary's house.

"Why are you so scared to tell Mary, love?" My dad asked as we drove away from our house.

I looked at him then, and feeling so tired and worn out said, "The more people I tell, Dad, the more real it becomes. I want to run away from it all, but wherever I go this will follow me, I feel trapped. The biggest decisions I make are what to wear on a night out with the girls, and now I will never get to go out again, my whole life will change forever."

He smiled then as he stopped the car at a traffic light and looked at me before saying, "I know it feels like that now love, but you are carrying my first grandchild in there and that baby is only going to bring more joy into our family. And you know, no matter what, that me, your mum and Carl will be here to help. You never know either, maybe Adam will too when you finally tell him. I don't want to overwhelm you, but whether you know it or not you will feel so much better when you know where you stand with him. He has a right to know and we will deal with whatever happens from there together."

Dad was always the voice of reason – one I was too scared to listen to right then, but I knew he wasn't wrong. He very rarely was.

"Anyway," he added, as we turned into Mary's estate, "let's get through one thing at a time."

We pulled up outside Mary's house and I didn't feel like I had the strength to even walk to the front door. It was all so emotionally draining being upset all the time, but I took one last deep breath and opened my dad's car door.

Here we go again! I thought.

It was becoming a bit of a habit with all the supportive people in my life to be at the front door with open arms – there Mary was! She didn't need to say anything, she just gave me the same hug that had become so familiar to me and said everything was going to be OK. Sweet cups of tea became the norm for me during that time and, cuppa in hand, my dad and I sat in Mary's sitting room with her and Mick, and I told them, through a lot of tears, how my life had changed in the last couple of weeks.

"Aoife, I know it feels like that now, and trust me I know exactly how overwhelmed you feel, but look at how much you have faced already. You have told all of the important people in your life and whether you realise it now or not you have created a support network around you so we are all here to help. I couldn't do that when I was pregnant with you and it just made things worse."

I had never felt so close to Mary as I did that day. She sat beside me, held my hand and I knew she truly understood what I was going through, because my exact path was her very own path twenty years before. She cried with me and made me feel accepted, not judged.

"I know how hard it must be for you to sit here and tell me this, and to have told your parents, but I am so proud of you for having the courage to do it."

"I was just so afraid of letting people down, you know?" I managed to say through my tissue. "I guess I am glad I told mum and dad as soon as I did because if I had left it longer I know it would have built up in my head and been so much harder, which is how I feel now about telling Adam. Maybe I should have told him as soon as I found out, at least then it would be over now, but I'm so scared and I don't know how I am ever going to find the courage to tell him now."

"Aoife, I wish I could sit here now and tell you that Adam is going to be there for you but I can't. What I can tell you is, whether or not he steps up to the plate, everything is still going to be OK. Things are so different now compared to when I was pregnant with you."

While stroking my hair she smiled and added, "Everything is going to be OK, I promise, but the sooner you tell him the better you will feel."

That is when I learned, for the first time that it is not about how you get knocked down; it's about getting back up again and never being ashamed to ask for help. That night my family helped me face the world again and when all is said and done, I believe everything happens for a reason. It was time for me to concentrate on that.

And yet again I found myself asking, *is it coincidence or fate that Mary had come into my life, right before the most life-changing event ever to happen to me?*

Chapter 14 – All by myself

I GOT myself together over the next couple of weeks and while I had my ups and downs, I was trying to stay positive. I had found my strength (most of the time) and one morning I woke up and finally felt able to tell Adam. I think, deep down, that I waited those few weeks because I knew what reaction I would get, but I also knew that it was something I would have to face, as it was only in the months previous that I found out my birth father never knew about me and I couldn't be responsible for that happening to my baby. Mary told me that she knew that John wouldn't be there, but knowing how I felt about the unknown in my life, I was adamant that I wouldn't make that decision. And so I vowed then to always do the right thing by my child, because I knew I would be looking him/her in the eye every day and would have to live with my decisions.

Again I called on Katherine to come for a drive with me. I would have been lost without my car, and without her for that matter! We drove up the mountains where we often went for a chat and Katherine talked me through what I was going to do and say. I drove and drove until we had nearly reached the top of the mountain, all the time knowing that when I stopped I would have to bite the bullet and phone him. I pulled my car over at a place called View Point, which has a beautiful view of Dublin city, and I slowly dialled his number. He answered straight away and my heart started to race.

What the hell? He had ignored me for weeks and now he answers straight way?

It took me a minute to even start speaking.

"Hello?"

"Hi, stranger, I haven't spoken to you in a while," I tried to start the conversation off with light-hearted tone.

"Yeah, sorry about that, you know me. I have had a lot going on with work and I haven't had any credit."

I didn't care about his excuses anymore, or that I had been fobbed off by him so many times, but as soon as I heard his voice I couldn't stand a minute longer of the small talk and so I launched right in.

"Listen, I was wondering if by any chance you were free to meet up this evening for a chat. There is something I wanted to speak to you about and I thought maybe the cafe on the corner beside you?"

He identified the nerves in my voice straight away and knew that something was up so quickly replied, "Is there something wrong? Aoife, just tell me now, I have to work tonight."

God, I really didn't want to do this over the phone, but I couldn't back out now and he wasn't leaving me with much choice. I tried once more to convince him.

"Honestly, Adam, it would mean a lot to me. I could meet you on your break, it won't take long."

I could see Katherine's face get angrier and angrier as she heard Adam's responses to me and eventually she whispered, "You just have to tell him."

And again, without warning, the words tumbled from my mouth.

"I'm pregnant."

I could hear the panic down the phone. Even his breathing changed.

"Are you messing?" were the first words he spoke to me.

I didn't even know how to answer that. It's not something a girl would mess around about.

"I can't believe this, I mean I can't do this," he was now an audible bag of nerves.

My heart sank. I knew he would be in shock but I was expecting even a little bit of consideration as to how I may have been feeling. Compassion, however, was not on the agenda – just blind panic.

"Are you sure the baby is mine?" he then asked.

With one sentence he had managed to break my heart. I knew we hadn't been in the most stable relationship in the world, but I never for one second would have considered he would question he was the father.

"Of course you are the father, I mean seriously? Do you really think I would be making this call now if I wasn't sure?"

I was angry, and he knew it.

"I have too much going on in my life, I have to be honest. I can't put my parents through this. Aoife, I can't do this!"

"It is not like I can choose who this baby's father is," I found the courage to say with my voice quivering. "But please don't leave me to face this on my own; this baby will be both our responsibilities."

I sat looking at the beautiful view of the city. It was so silent up there, no other people, no other cars, just us, and I watched the shadows get bigger across the fields as I heard Adam say the words that cut like a knife and would haunt me for a long time.

"You will find someone to be a much better father to that child than I could ever be."

There was silence as I imagined my jaw dropping to the floor.

"You will find someone to be a much better father to that child than I could ever be." I repeated back to him before words simply failed me.

I sat in my car staring at the autumn leaves falling on my windscreen and it felt like time stood still. I will never forget the pain it caused to hear him say it. *What type of a man could say that about his own child? Could he really mean that? Maybe it was just the shock?*

I couldn't stand to speak to him after that and finished the conversation by saying, "Adam please think about what you are saying, what you would be giving up here… your child. I know it is a shock. It is for me too, but please just think about things before you decide. This decision will affect so many other lives, not just your own."

"OK, I will think about it, but seriously I can't do this, not now. I have to go to work".

Still in shock I said goodbye and he quickly hung up the phone.

Katherine was also in shock. She had met Adam a few times and had always thought he was a nice guy – yet here she was watching as her best friend tried to convince him to acknowledge his own baby. I could see the disbelief and anger in her face, but she didn't say a word. She just gave me a hug as I cried and repeated over and over, "I can't do this on my own. How can I be a single mother? I am not strong enough."

I heard from Adam a few times over the following weeks, but I never got any support or answers from him after that day. I had, however, slowly become stronger during that time, thanks to all of the love and support I had been getting from my family and friends and I began to realise that I didn't need him in order for me to be a good mummy. I wasn't going to be a good mummy because he was there; I was going to be a good mummy despite the fact that he wasn't there.

I was feeling good about myself and my new found strength, but I still hadn't got over the feeling that I wanted my child to have, not just a father, but a daddy. There would be times in life when no matter how strong I was for my child, I wouldn't be able to take the place or fill the shoes of a loving caring daddy. At times my concerns changed to embarrassment, because although I had come to terms with having my baby alone and I loved my unborn child unconditionally already, I was still a young twenty-year-old girl and like most girls my age, I cared what people thought. I began to dread going to my hospital appointments, beside all the happy families but looking like a lost little girl in the corner. It was the same hospital that Mary had left me in twenty years before too.

I found it hard not to get caught up in that part of it and felt like everyone was looking at me wherever I went – although I'm sure now that was all in my head. Through it all though, no matter how hard it was for me, my mum was there at every appointment helping me to hold my head up. She was there so I wouldn't be alone.

Those few months were a whirlwind of emotions, working me up into believing that I could do this, and that I'd be fine. One minute I would feel confident and the next so scared, but the one thing I did know was that no matter how concerned I was, there was no running away from it.

The going got tough, but for the first time in my life I had to stay and face the music.

Time was passing fast though and even though strength was fleeting in its visits to me, and I had to convince myself to get up and face the world every day, I woke up one morning to a change. I knew very quickly that this particular day was going to be different. Something didn't feel right and I raced to the bathroom and discovered I was bleeding. There it was in an instant, my moment of clarity. The one I had been searching for over the past three months. In one split second all of the confusion was gone and all of the tears and fear didn't matter anymore. Alone or not, single parent or not, it really didn't matter. All that mattered from that second on was that all of my priorities had changed and it seemed easy. I wanted my baby. I needed my baby to be OK more than I had ever needed anything in my whole life. They say sometimes you don't know what you have until it's gone (or nearly lose it in my case) and that was the day that my instinct as a parent kicked in. From then on it got me through and has never left me. The love I had for my child, even if I never had anything else, would be enough.

Thank God, after a race to the hospital, I learned from a scan that my baby was fine and I felt like I could breathe again. It didn't matter anymore that I was sitting in the waiting room surrounded by happy loving couples. It didn't even matter whether my baby had a cooperative father or not. My baby had me and I was not going to let him or her down now. I will always be grateful for that day, because without it I may have taken longer to pull myself out of the self-pity stage and realise that I was going to be a mummy. That to me, when all is said and done, is the most amazing gift I could ever receive.

Everything happens for a reason and even the hard days are a part of your journey – the one that will eventually turn you into the person you are meant to be.

My social life changed a lot during my pregnancy and I went from every Friday night being out with the girls to being in with my folks watching *The Late Late Show* in my PJs. One Friday night, however, my friends called and tried to convince me to come out with them. They were telling me just because I was pregnant didn't mean that I had to stay in all the time, so I took their advice and drove us all to the pub. I had said I would only stay for a couple of orange juices and then leave them to it, but it was good to get out and do something normal again.

I was about six months pregnant at this stage and was queuing at the bar when I met a friend who I hadn't seen in ages. She was also a friend of Adam's and came straight over to congratulate me on my pregnancy. She then told me something that hurt me more than I ever imagined. She said that she had met Adam a couple of weeks before and said to him that she had heard that I was having a baby, and his answer to this was, "That is the first I have heard of it!"

I was crushed, despite myself. He had been in touch with me on and off and gave me the impression that, although I knew I couldn't rely on him, that he just needed time. He had even, more recently to this, seemed to be coming around to the idea a little – although, I was realising, maybe that was just what I had wanted to think. I knew now that he had obviously not told anyone else in his life, not even friends, let alone his family. I couldn't believe how wrong I been about him and I felt like a fool having even given him the chance to hurt me that way.

He was leaving me totally alone to deal with all of this and I felt more let down that night than I did the first night I told him. But it wouldn't be long before I was given the opportunity to confront him about what I heard, because later that same night he strolled by me in the pub. I think he got a shock when he saw my big pregnant belly and it seemed real to him for the first time. I knew by the way he was staring at me but I was just so hurt and marched over to him saying, "I can't believe you haven't told anybody. Do you think all this is going to go away just because you don't tell anyone?"

"What is wrong with you?" he casually replied, as if he hadn't a clue what I was talking about.

I was furious.

"I am going to be having this baby sooner rather than later and you still haven't told your parents that they are going to have a grandchild? That is insane. I mean whether or not you are dealing with this, do you not think they have the right to know?"

"I don't mean to make things harder for you," he replied. "But I told you before it has been a hard few years at home and I can't do this to my mum at the minute. It doesn't mean you can't call me if you need anything. I just don't want to speak about it to anyone else yet. Understand that I just need time."

I didn't know whether or not to believe him. It is hard to face the reality when you have even a glimmer of hope, but I do know that I wanted to believe him so that clouded my judgement. The alternative was to face up to the harsh reality that I would now, most definitely, be having this baby on my own. No thanks. If there was any chance of a positive outcome I was going to hold on to it even, if it was just because I wouldn't feel so scared.

One thing I did know was that I was getting closer and closer to having the baby and he wouldn't have an endless amount of time to find his courage. We spoke less after that conversation and I carried on as I had been – on my own.

Weeks turned into months and before long there were just a couple of weeks left in my pregnancy. Real friends always tell you the truth so I had stopped speaking about Adam to them because I couldn't face another "You will be better off on your own" conversation. I was still trying to avoid that reality at all costs. As it turned out I had to spend the last few weeks in hospital because my blood pressure was high. Mum and dad came in to see me every day and my friends too, bringing in all the latest magazines so I wouldn't get bored. I had come to terms with doing this on my own but I'd be lying if I didn't say I still had hope that when his child was born, Adam would want to be a part of his/her life.

After a few days in hospital I was relaxing on the bed when I got a text. Adam's name appeared on the screen.

I am having a quiet night. Bored, do you fancy meeting up?

So casual, as if nothing negative had ever happened between us. I hadn't told him I was in hospital because he hadn't been involved.

So I replied. *I know we haven't spoken in a while, is there any reason in particular you want to see me? Have you had a chance to think?*

I couldn't take my eyes off the screen, hoping with all of my heart that he had finally came to his senses and wanted to see me to tell me he had told his family and would be there for his child.

Typically however, his response was, *No news, just thought you would fancy a drive or something.*

When was I going to stop hoping for him to do the right thing?

Get a grip, Aoife I thought to myself.

My answer was short.

I am in hospital.

I don't know what I expected his response to be, but I had hoped it would be one of even slight concern, if not for me for the baby, but he didn't even ask if we were OK and bluntly replied, *Let me know if you can get out for an hour.*

I stared at my phone in disbelief. Did he really care that little? It was a new low, even for him. I tried to hold myself together and not get upset. I was on a ward with other pregnant ladies and didn't want anybody to see me cry – I knew it wouldn't do my blood pressure any good either – but I couldn't help it and once I started I couldn't stop. I wasn't crying because I knew he didn't care for me. It was the thought that anyone could care so little about their own child that cut deep. I was annoyed with myself too for letting him hurt me again. It wasn't long before a passing nurse noticed my tears and the state I was getting myself into and she came over to try and comfort me. I couldn't even get the words out when she asked me why I was so upset so I just sat there like a blubbering mess with mascara running down my face and she just pulled up a chair beside me and held my hand.

A small gesture of kindness from this lovely young nurse was more comfort and support than I had got from Adam in nine months.

Chapter 15 – The day my life changed

THE day finally arrived when the doctors told me that they thought I had been pregnant for long enough and wanted to induce my labour. For some reason I wasn't scared that day. I had been scared for so long and experienced every possible emotion over the previous nine months that I was drained from it and just wanted to meet my baby. A baby that may be born into a world with just one parent present, but I would be one parent that would love it more than anything. A parent that would work as hard as it took to make my child happy, safe and secure.

Mum came in to see me as usual that day, not expecting it to be the day where everything swung into action and she got a shock to see me hooked up to the foetal monitor with contractions already in full swing. I hadn't called her when they started me because I didn't feel like that lost little girl at that precise moment in time. I felt like a woman who was about to become a mummy.

I think I had blinkers on to the world that day. Maybe it was a self-preservation method, but I found strength I never knew was in me and I knew that all I had to focus on was bringing my baby into the world safety. I didn't even think about Adam, or about telling him because I knew that I would just feel let down and upset when he didn't show. Besides, that day was not about him. I refused to let it be. I finally knew that I didn't need him.

Mum was by my bed all day long getting me ice cubes and holding my hand; as she also tried to keep me occupied and distracted by reading interesting articles from the paper. I don't think she knew what else to do, because she may have two children but she had never experienced labour, which was one of the reasons I had asked her to be with me.

She may not have been there when her son or daughter came into the world but to be there when her first grandchild was born I knew would be so special for her, and for me. By six o'clock I was in a lot of pain. The contractions were on top of each other and very strong. I had laboured all that day without any pain relief so I asked (or should I say begged) mum to go and get the nurse for me – I just felt like I couldn't do anymore. The nurse, however, came and told me that I was close to having my baby and that it was time to go to the delivery room. I never thought I'd make the walk down that long corridor. I was finding it so tough and had never experienced pain like it, so when I eventually made it there, after stopping every twenty seconds during a contraction and holding on to mum, I asked for an epidural which they got me fairly quickly.

My beautiful son was finally born, weighing 7 pounds, 15 ounces, at 7.45pm. The moment the little bundle, with blonde hair and blue eyes, was placed in my arms, in a blue hospital blanket, was a moment that will stay with me for the rest of my life. Holding my hand tighter than ever before mum looked at me holding my little boy. "You're a mummy, my baby is a mummy," she beamed. "You have done so well today I am so proud of you and look at this gorgeous little guy! He looks just like you did."

I loved my son with all that I had and he was only five minutes old. The nurse was arranging his clothes to get him dressed and she asked me if I had a name for him. I looked at my mum, who had the biggest smile I had ever seen, and I introduced her to her grandson.

"This is Jack." I named him after my dad's father, my Papa Jack. I had never known a man I respected more than my dad and I knew my son would be proud to have a name from his side of the family.

*

While I was in labour, my parents had phoned Mary so she could come to the hospital and be there when Jack was born. I stayed in the delivery room for about an hour with my new little baby boy, having the nicest tea and toast I had ever tasted, while mum went to the waiting room to tell everyone the news.

I knew she couldn't wait to be the one that made that big announcement and I was delighted for her. In the meantime I just sat there staring into my son's eyes and for those few minutes the rest of the world didn't exist. He lay there quietly looking up at me with his hand holding on to my finger with such strength. I was in love. I never knew that much love was possible, a love that, I know now, only a parent can understand. I glanced around the room and for the first time my son and I were alone.

"I am your mummy, and I already love you, Jack, more than anything in the world. You gave me a hard time today; I'm hoping that won't be a sign of things to come." I smiled and added, "I am your mummy, my beautiful boy. It is me and you against the world." The nurse came into the room then, full of smiles telling me I did a great job and it was time to go up to the ward. I had my special few moments with my beautiful new baby and now it was time to introduce him to the family.

She wheeled me up to the lift and we travelled up to level five. As soon as the lift doors opened there stood my dad, my brother and Mary all waiting for me with the biggest look of excitement on their faces. Dad was going snap happy with his camera and Mary came up, with tears in her eyes, to tell me how proud she was of me. I couldn't help but think how hard it must have been for her, to see me there holding my baby in the same hospital she had given birth to me in – the same hospital in which she left me.

We arrived at my room and I noticed that there were four other ladies in there too, but only three other babies. One of the beds had an empty cot beside a young girl looking lost and alone.

"I wonder where her baby is," I whispered to mum.

The sight of this clean white room, full of so much happiness, with new mothers, babies, balloons and cards everywhere, all of a sudden seemed so sad with this poor girl in the corner desperately trying not to make eye contact with me as I was wheeled in holding my new baby son. I may not have thought nine months ago that I was ready to have a baby, but I had my beautiful bundle here with me now and he had already given me so much joy – yet here was this poor girl with nothing to look at but her own empty arms. Her bed was across from mine so I pulled the curtain around me as I got settled, so as not to rub our joy in her face.

I hope I will get a chance to speak to her later, I thought to myself, as everyone had a cuddle with the newest member of the family. Soon it was time for mum, dad and Carl to leave and make their way home. They had been in the hospital all day and so Mary and I were eventually left alone.

She couldn't take her eyes off me holding my baby boy and as they filled with tears she said, "Well, you have done it and I couldn't be prouder of you."

I smiled and answered, "I knew it would be hard, but now that he is here somehow it doesn't seem to matter anymore. Look at him isn't he perfect?"

Mary reached out to hold my hand.

"Ten little fingers and ten little toes," she said.

A nurse popped her head around the curtain then, with a ready-made bottle in her hand.

"I think this little guy is ready for his first feed, what do you think mum, ready to give it a go?"

I looked at Mary and then down at Jack in my arms. Still she hadn't taken her eyes off him. I knew she was looking at him thinking about all the things she had missed out on with me – things like giving me my first bottle and it was then that it came to me.

Awkwardly, I shuffled myself towards the edge of the bed and gently placed my brand new baby boy in Mary's arms before holding out the bottle for her to take.

"Time to move forward," I said. "We don't have to miss any more big events in each other's lives; I would love you to give my son his first bottle."

Shocked and overjoyed it was the first time that Mary could not find words. She didn't even try to wipe the tears away as they streamed down her face and I knew, at that moment, that it was the most meaningful gift I could ever have given her.

It was a real full circle moment, one neither of us will ever forget. She was creating the most special memories for me as I looked at her feed Jack and we didn't speak at all – she spent the whole time talking to her grandson. She finally got to have that special moment that had been denied to her when I was born. She finally got to say all the things, as she looked into Jack's eyes, that she had been so eager to say to me when we were both in this place the first time around.

I spent the next three days in hospital recovering and getting to know my son. Every now and then thoughts of the girl across the room, still with no baby, would enter my head. She didn't speak to anyone and I didn't want to make her feel uncomfortable but I wondered constantly where her baby was. I hoped the baby wasn't sick. I also considered that maybe she was giving the child up for adoption. I simply didn't know, but I saw the pain of whatever had happened written all over her face.

I knew what it was like to feel that alone. Now that I had my son, however, I knew I never would be again and that lifted me more than anyone ever had. On the last day my parents came in to bring me home from the hospital and as I was walking towards the door a baby in a tiny little cot was wheeled by me. Looking over my shoulder I was so relieved as I got to see the pain instantly melt away from that poor girl's face as she was reunited with her child. I turned to walk down the long hallway, satisfied now, and ready to bring my baby home.

As I sat in the back of the car, driving through Dublin, I watched the world go by with different eyes. I was looking at everything differently now, it seemed. We eventually drove into the driveway. It was a beautiful sunny day and I was delighted to see Carl waiting at the front door on the step. I knew he had wanted to be the one to bring Jack through it for the first time, usually the job of the new daddy, but between us we were making sure Jack didn't miss out on any special moments – and having a loving uncle bring him home was the next best thing.

Carl

I often think back on it - it was a cold and wet November evening when the very idea of Jack first entered my awareness. Still in my work clothes, I'd been relaxing on the couch in my apartment, entirely unprepared for the imminent bombshell... The doorbell rang and I got to my feet to answer the intercom. It was one of those old 90s intercoms with a grainy TV screen and as the black and white picture very slowly came into focus, what I could see standing out in the rain was my very distressed and emotional sister. Without hesitation, I buzzed her in and she took the elevator three stories up to where I was ready-

ing myself for whatever devastation she had in store.

My mind quickly busied itself, envisioning all worst case scenarios and possibilities. Car crashes, deaths, disasters. What was it that could have her so upset? Had something happened to mam or da? I brought her in and we hurried into the living room. She looked like she needed a seat!

"What is it? What has you like this?" I asked, hand on her shoulder, gently trying to tease out of her this great burden that she seemed to be carrying.

"Carl.., I'm.., I'm pregnant," she sobbed.

There was a brief pause before I erupted with laughter. I don't think I've ever had a more relieving, deep bellyache of a laugh. Aoife's forehead crumpled with confusion as she tried to work out what was going on.

"What..... what...", she was lost for words...

"Jesus, I thought you were going to tell me Max was dead!" I explained through fits and snorts. I really loved that dog (still miss him, too!). We'd had him since I was eight and he was getting on in years.

Looking back on it, of course this reaction was entirely inappropriate, but how often in life are you going to be confronted with some horrible, devastating truth? More than once, that's for certain. Probably twice, and that's if you're lucky, and there we were, trying to come to terms with a new life being brought in to the world. Worse things have most definitely happened and at the risk of sounding callous, Aoife wasn't the first young woman to find herself in this predicament. Who cared about what people would think or say, anyway?

Not long after, I moved home to help out. I'm pretty sure the time flew by. I remember planning and practicing routes to Holles Street and, bizarrely, going with her to see Eminem in Punchestown a couple of days before the due date. Myself and the lads had a super-sized designated driver to bring us all home that night!

What wasn't easy however, was the post-natal depression. I reckon it must've been going on for quite a while before we clocked it. Looking back a decade on, it's fascinating to think about the complete distortion in cognition and logic that she'd continually show (yes, even more so than usual!). For that time, the family home wasn't the most comfortable place to inhabit, but she (and we) eventually got through it. Through even the simple awareness of its presence, steps can be gently taken to make the depression manageable, until one day it's simply not there anymore and all that's left is the greatest little nephew an uncle could imagine.

*

It was the day that the thoughts of telling Adam crept back into my head. For my son's sake I decided that I wanted to leave the door open for him to be a part of his life and if he decided that he didn't want to then at least I would always know that I had done my bit. Most importantly I could look into my son's eyes and tell him I did everything I could to make it easy for his father to be involved. Being able to tell Jack the truth and as much information as he wanted when he was old enough, was the most important thing to me. I had learned that lesson the hard way.

So I rang Adam and, surprise surprise, he didn't answer. Maybe he was afraid to hear that the waiting was over and he now had a child. I decided though that all I could do was what I had control over, so I said that I would send him a text and then forget about it for the day. It was my son's first day at home and I didn't have room in my head for anything other than joy.

I tried to phone you, but again didn't get through. I thought that you would like to know that you have a son. Everything went well and he is fit and healthy. We came home today if you would like to meet him.

I felt a wave of sadness wash over me as I watched the message send. It was a lot to get my head around, the fact that my son's father had created a situation where he decided to find out that he had a child by text, but I guessed that was the way it had to be and I was doing all I could.

I wasn't expecting a reply, but to my surprise I received one straight away as I sat in my mum's kitchen with my baby in my arms.

Ha-ha that is great news, what is his name? How big was he? I am happy that everything went well.

I could never get inside his head and I never knew what he was thinking. It was sent as though it was the most normal text in the world. As if he had nothing to do with this child. I had received more meaningful messages from people in college, ones I had only known a year.

I have named him Jack and I would be happy to bring him to meet you. I replied.

I'm sure I will soon.

That was it, I didn't see the point in responding to that so I left him be. I had a baby to look after now.

I didn't get a minute to myself to enjoy my new baby that day, my phone never stopped and the doorbell was constantly ringing. I was so grateful for everyone's well wishes and support but I couldn't wait until it was just Jack and I. We needed our time. My parents eventually helped me up the stairs, with everything we would need to get through our first night together, then they said goodnight and shut the door behind them.

"I guess it is just you and me kid," I said, as I watched him sleep so peacefully in my arms. My thoughts were finally my own, my phone was quiet and I could not hear a sound from mum or dad downstairs. This was what I had been longing for all day, so why all of a sudden was I feeling so sad? So overwhelmed! It hit me in that split second that I had not got a clue what I was doing, and that was the start of my depression.

In the weeks that followed I tried to get into the swing of bottles and sterilisers, night feeds and nappies. It was very hard taking on all of these tasks with me being the only person responsible for Jack, but I did get a lot of help from my parents and they helped me with the feeds too, or if I had a bad night mum would take Jack for the morning so I could get some sleep. I knew how lucky I was but I still couldn't shake this feeling that I wasn't a very good mum.

Before I knew it, Jack was eight weeks old. Adam had been in touch by text a few times but there was never any mention of setting up a time for him to meet his son. It was always "I will," but it never happened.

Then one afternoon I was out bringing Jack for a walk in the park and showing him the dogs playing in the field, with my friend and her baby, when again my phone beeped and I saw a message from Adam.

Just so you know I am going away for a few months, out of the country, and I am leaving on Saturday.

He really did feel like he didn't owe his son, or me for that matter, anything. Was I supposed to feel honoured that he took the time to tell me? My only response back to him was, *Are you not going to come and meet your son before you go?*

To which he replied, *I have a really busy few days packing and meeting people, but I will try my best.*

Nothing that he did shocked me anymore. My friends were going crazy, but I had come to expect nothing less. All I felt was sorrow for Jack. I didn't text Adam back after that and just went on about my normal life as usual that week, all the while thinking to myself, *if he doesn't meet his son before he goes I don't think he ever will.*

That Friday evening, at eight o'clock, I was at home after being around in Clare's house helping her to decide what to wear for the usual Friday night get together that I could no longer be a part of. It was September so the sun was going down behind the trees and I was getting Jack ready for bed when my phone rang. It was Adam. As usual he acted as if he was just ringing a friend for a chat until I stopped him in his tracks.

"How can you live with what you are doing, to never even have seen your son's face?"

Then he shocked me.

"Can you come meet me with Jack in Naas?"

I didn't know what to say or what to think so I just agreed.

"I haven't got much time to spare and I am up to my eyes packing, but I don't want to leave things up in the air."

"I am so glad you think that, just wait until you see him. It will change everything, he is perfect – just wait and see. I will see you soon," I said eagerly.

I drove to Naas that night, so nervous, with Jack crying for the entire journey. Normally he was good in the car but maybe that night he felt the tension. I didn't even know where we were going to meet Adam, I just said I would phone when we got to the big Naas ball and he directed me to a housing estate beside a garage, off the main road, then into the town. When I got there I pulled in and was about to phone him when he pulled up behind me. He was about to meet his son, who was already two months old, for the first time on the side of the road. None of it made any sense to me, but I had to get on with it so I said nothing as he climbed into the passenger seat. I then got out and took Jack out of his seat before bringing him in beside me and shutting the car door – locking the world out.

Adam just sat there in silence and stared at him.

"This is Jack, Adam. This is your son."

I passed the baby over for him to hold.

I had imagined this moment so many times in my head, but it was nothing like what I had hoped for. I watched as Adam looked at Jack and I could see no emotion.

"Well little man, how are you doing? I heard you have some set of lungs on you are you hungry?" he said as he picked up a bottle and began to feed him.

There were no apologies or any emotion, he just talked to Jack and told me about his trip.

"I need you to think about your involvement in Jack's life when you are away," I pressed. "I am assuming you still haven't told your family? How can you look your son in the eyes, hold him in your arms, yet still deny him at the same time? I want to understand but can't."

Adam didn't respond but I saw this as my only chance to try and make him see. To try and push him to do the right thing for his son, so I wasn't going to hold back, not now.

"The longer you leave this the more of a big deal it will be and they've already missed out on so much in his life – as have you."

Again Adam stayed silent and simply nodded at me in agreement. When he eventually did speak I knew he was upset.

"Can you email me some pictures of Jack when I am away? I have to go," he said as he placed Jack back into my arms.

All I cared about was doing right by my son and I was happy that I could now tell him that I had tried my best, whatever way it worked out. I drove home in dead silence. Jack was sleeping and I felt a whole mess of emotions. Happy that my son had met his father and sad that it had to come to this, knowing that it may be the first and only time they would ever see each other.

Over the coming months I heard from Adam a few times, most of the time it wasn't ever about Jack. I emailed the photos that he had asked me to send before he left but he never asked for Jack and when that became a common theme I didn't feel the need to respond anymore. If he wasn't going to be responsible in relation to his child then, I thought, we had nothing else to talk about. I had hoped I had gotten through to him that night in Naas. I had hoped that Jack had gotten through to him, but the more time that passed, the more unlikely that seemed. I was never nasty to him; I just didn't want us to act as if we hadn't got this huge unresolved history and permanent connection.

After he was gone around five months I received an email with the subject matter JACK. I guess he thought that would get my attention. He told me that he was coming home in four weeks and was afraid of what he would come home to.

I think in the back of his mind he thought that people would find out or I would tell his family what he hadn't the courage to himself. His own actions were what had made the whole situation so unmanageable for him and now he didn't know which way to turn, or how to face it. Well, I wasn't about to tell him that everything was going to be ok or give him the reassurance he was looking for, because I wouldn't have been true to my child if I did that. Besides I couldn't make everything ok. That was down to him. He had to face his family and his child; I couldn't do that for him.

I began to type my response in a million and one different ways but I eventually deleted my massive rant, after reminding myself that this wasn't about me anymore, it was about Jack, and started again.

Hi Adam,

I hope you have had a good trip. I am more than happy for you to come and see Jack once you have arrived home. I won't, however, be bringing him back out of the house again at bedtime for you to see him at the side of the road. If you would like to see him you can come over to our house where Jack is comfortable. You don't need to worry about me telling your family because that is something you are going to have to face. All I can do is concentrate on Jack. I will speak to you about it when you get home if you like.

You can let me know what you decide.

Aoife

He had been home about a week when I got an answer by text.

Hi. I was wondering if you were free this afternoon to meet up. I don't really want to go where your family will be around though.

I wasn't surprised. He hadn't got the courage to face them before so I wasn't expecting now to be any different.

Fair enough, Adam, we need to talk so you can come over to my house, mum and dad are in work for the afternoon so it will be just Jack and I here. I finished college early today, so just give me an hour. I am on my way to pick him up from the crèche.

The last time Adam saw Jack he was a tiny little baby but by then he was about eight months old and walking with the help of one of those children's walking toys – a huge milestone in the life of a baby. Adam, however, didn't even know what crèche his son was in.

The doorbell rang and I picked Jack up in my arms and we went to answer it together.

"Hi, come on in."

I had never seen him so nervous before, but he came in, sat on the floor and started playing with Jack. I think he was looking for a distraction, anything but look me in the eye.

"Do you want to show me your toys Jack?" Adam said awkwardly to his son.

Jack brought over his toys to show him, but again I saw no emotion in his eyes.

"Why are you here Adam? Has anything changed?" I finally asked.

"To be honest I still don't know how I feel," he said half-heartedly, as he raced Jack's favourite toy car around the floor in front of him. "I am confused," he continued. "I might not always feel this way but I just want you to give me time to figure it out in my head."

I was livid.

"Give you more time?" I demanded. "Do you just want me to stop Jack from growing up until you figure it out?"

I knew getting angry wasn't going to do anyone any favours but this was too much, he was the priority in his own life, not me and not Jack, and I was fed up.

I sat there listening to him blame his job for not being able to come and see Jack all the time, what a cop out, and I realised that I was looking into the face of a coward – one who there was little chance of ever changing. I knew then that we would never get what we needed from him and as quick as he had come he was gone.

I sat on the floor with my son as I realised we had both been sitting down with a stranger. Jack didn't know him as his daddy and I could not introduce him as that. *What was I doing? How long was I going to be so stupid for?* It was time to face the harsh reality that my son was without a daddy, and possibly always would be.

Adam didn't come and see Jack voluntarily after that. There was just one more time, a few months later, when I randomly bumped into him in a shop and told him that Jack was outside in the car with my friend if he wanted to come and see him, which he did for two minutes, popping his head in through the window.

"Hello little man!"

Jack just started crying because he didn't know who this strange man was.

We had contact on and off, after that but that was how it was left in relation to Jack. No more questions asked, no more answers given and it was after that day that reality really set in for me.

I know, looking back, that it had been obvious, right from the start, that it would be Jack and me on our own. Somehow at the time though, I guess as long as Adam and I still had contact I still had hope that he would be there. Stupid, I know, but that is how I got through it. It was so important to me that Jack had a father in his life, that somewhere along the way I lost track of reality and sight of the hard fact that only he could decide if he was going to be a father to him. I couldn't force him or try to guilt him into it, or wait until he was "ready." It was time for me to accept things the way they were.

I got upset at this final realisation and I found I was angry with myself for letting things continue in limbo for as long as I did, but my mum, as usual, talked me down.

"That is just who you are Aoife, you always want to see the good in people. I hope you will find somebody one day who will love you for you and somebody who recognises how special your little boy is and love him for who he is too. But for the moment, it is time for you to concentrate on your son and yourself."

She was right. I had made Jack a promise on the day that he was born, that no matter what, I would do whatever it took to make sure he had a happy, safe and secure life and it was now that I was going to concentrate on making sure that happened. I was going to give my son somebody to be proud of.

That somebody was me.

Clare

From the day Aoife told me she was pregnant I worried about her. I knew she was strong but we were so young and this was huge. We went for drives a lot, just to get away from it all and chat. The day we went on one of our favourite drives up to View Point, in the Dublin Mountains, was a day I will never forget. That was the day Aoife asked me to be her unborn child's Godmother. I was honoured and I took it so seriously. It looked like there may not be a daddy in this little baby's life but between all the people who loved Aoife we were going to make sure that he/she had all the love they needed. I tried to go to hospital appointments with her and it made our bond even stronger. I also went to her final prenatal class with her because most people were bringing husbands and boyfriends for support. They were showing a video one day of a baby being born and I have to admit it scared the life out of both of us, but there was nowhere else I wanted to be. I knew how hard she was finding it and in my eyes being asked to be her baby's Godmother, especially in her situation, was a big responsibility but one that I was happy to undertake.

When I finally got the chance to hold my new Godson in my arms I was so proud of her for what she had achieved and I just knew in that moment that she was going to be ok. Watching her change so much, in such a short period of time, was surreal. She went from a young carefree girl to a new mummy and it wasn't long before I realised, looking at her, that we were not kids ourselves anymore.

Chapter 16 – In the army now

JACK and I were doing OK by ourselves, but even though I had gone back to finish college in an effort to try and get my life back on track, I have to be honest – we weren't really going it alone. Mum was still doing a lot of the hard work for me. When I couldn't face bringing him to the doctor for his injections my mum did, when I was too tired to stay up in the morning, mum did, and when I decided it was all too much to keep going mum was there to hold his hand.

Jack's christening day was coming up and I was dreading it. I had become used to the looks of pity from people watching me raise my son by myself and although I knew they were coming from a good place when they would say things like, "I don't know how you do it, it must be so hard," I didn't want anyone's pity. I was racked with guilt too that what they didn't know was that my mum was behind the scenes keeping everything from falling apart.

I would be lying if I said I didn't feel sad getting Jack all dressed up for church on the day. My folks loved him just as much as I did, and he loved them, but the thought of him not having a daddy there to love him too just meant it wasn't the same – there was something missing and because of that it became another day I just wanted to get through and get over with.

Clare and Carl were his Godparents so they were both sitting in the front row with me. There were no other babies getting christened that day because we had organised a family friend to christen Jack.

The cold church soon filled with all of my friends and family and I didn't realise how many people had come until it was time to bring Jack up to the water and I faced everyone. With my eyes brimming with tears I looked around the room then and saw all of their lovely faces. No pity, no judge-mental stares, just so much warmth, joy, love and support. I realised in that moment, that for the first time ever I had both of my families, all in the same place at the same time and coming together to celebrate Jack, a new addition. Standing on that alter, looking down at all of them, I finally real-ised that I was never, and will never, be alone, and neither would Jack. After all, some two-parent families were not half as lucky as my son and I were to have all of that love and support in their lives, and in the end it made for one truly special day.

*

I became obsessed with the idea, over the coming months, of making Jack proud of his mummy. I wanted to find something that would teach me to be strong so I could get through it on my own, and I lay in my bed night after night watching my son sleep while racking my brains. It had to be something big, something that scared me, something that my mum couldn't be there to hold my hand for. Then one night, at about 2am, it hit me. I was going to become a soldier.

I needed something. I had a lot of friends in the army and their families were proud of them so that must be it!

It quickly became all that I was focusing on. I wasn't expecting it to be easy, but that was the point, it had to be something I worked hard at to achieve. The process involved an interview and then, if you passed that, a medical after which you entered the last stage, which was a fitness test.

I soon realised the extent of the commitment required when I was told that my training would involve living away from home for at least six months.

But how would I live away from Jack?

I realised how ironic it sounded, but in order to stop leaning on my parents and take on the world as a single parent I had to ask them one last favour. The biggest favour I have ever asked anyone… I had to ask them to become parents to my son. I could not leave him with anyone else.

I didn't know how I could leave him at all. I couldn't normally leave him for a weekend without feeling guilty, but that didn't stop me because in my heart I was doing it for him. I had tunnel vision. A feeling that I had to do something big for our future together and this was as big as it got.

It was around the time of Jack's first birthday and I had done all of my research before I sat down with my parents to tell them about what I felt I needed to do. Mum and dad were both chatting over a coffee in the kitchen when I came down the stairs after putting Jack to bed. My dad placed a sweet cup of tea down in front of me and I couldn't help but think he had a sense that there was something up. Tea was always the sign in our house that a big conversation was about to happen.

"Mum, dad I need to speak to you both if you have a sec," I said from behind my giant mug.

They both looked up at me and waited for me to continue.

"I have been doing a lot of thinking and I can't rely on you guys forever, I have a son now and I still feel like a little girl myself. I am finishing up in college in a few months and then what? How am I ever going to support Jack? Jobs in the media are so hard to find, especially with no experience outside college so I need a job that will pay and give us security."

My dad smiled at me, no doubt thinking to himself, *my little girl is finally growing up,* but he had no idea of what was coming.

"I have been doing a lot of research and…. I don't know how to say this without sounding horrible so I'm just going to spit it out…"

Mum raised her eyebrows, but didn't say a word.

"I want to join the army!"

I was expecting a reaction, a bad one. But I got no reaction at all.

"I want to join the army so I can give Jack the life he deserves. The only thing is that, just for the initial six months, I would have to live in the barracks, which would mean leaving Jack."

As soon as I said the words "leaving Jack" out loud I couldn't even believe what I was saying.

God I bet they are going to go mad, I thought.

Mum looked at dad, but neither of them spoke a word for what felt like an eternity. Finally, though she glanced up at my dad and he nodded his head to her before she took a deep breath.

"Aoife, I don't know why on earth you feel like you have something to prove, you are a new mum and you are learning just like we all had to. Things will fall into place, you don't always have to have everything perfect right this second, these things take time."

"I know, Mum," I said. "I know they take time, but how can I ever even be headed in the right direction if I don't do something now to change my life?"

Dad decided it was time to speak up.

"I thought you had gotten over that stage of running away from life. You have been doing so well, facing up to everything. Don't run now."

"Don't you see, Dad? This is me facing up to life, a life I need to build for my son by myself." My voice trailed off and there was silence.

But as the last sip of coffee left mum's lips she looked at me again and said, "We will step out of the grandparent role, and into a parent one. We will do all the night feeds and deal with the tantrums. I just hope you know what you are doing because you need those hugs from that little boy every day, just as much as he does."

My dad nodded, adding, "We will support you if this is something you really feel is right."

And I did. I really felt it was going to take something drastic to turn my life around and this was my chance. They knew it was a crazy idea but they let me do what I felt I needed to for Jack and, as a parent, as hard as it may be, sometimes you have to let your kids make their own mistakes…

*

It all started with an interview in Cathal Brugha barracks. I was so nervous walking up to the big iron gates that day, but I was so determined to get away from feeling like that lost little girl that I forced myself to be brave. I didn't want to feel vulnerable anymore.

It wasn't long before I was called into the room and I found myself standing in front of three soldiers who were sitting behind a long desk. They were friendly and welcoming, but it really was one of the most intimidating moments of my life. I felt like I held my nerve well and got through the interview OK, but to be honest, I couldn't wait to get out of there so I could breathe. They told me that I would find out within a week, through the post, if I had progressed through to the next stage, so I went home and waited for the postman.

Five days had passed when he finally approached the front door and dropped the letter through the post box and into the hall. Jack always had the job of racing out to the door and bringing the post in and this morning was no different. He came back into the room with four letters, one of which was addressed to me and I knew instantly that this was it. I was almost afraid to look inside, but took a deep breath and slowly teased the envelope open.

I had passed my interview and they were giving me a time and date to report for a medical at army hospital!

This was my time to do something good with my life, to make my son proud, and the medical day soon came around. I wasn't as nervous that day and went through hours of tests along with the other potential recruits. It wasn't a surprise to me to hear that I had passed my medical as I knew I was in good health and hadn't any issues, but it was getting real now and the last stage of the process was all down to me. I had to prove my fitness.

I knew the test was going to involve a mile and a half run, which I had to complete in less than thirteen minutes, and this made me nervous – the one thing that I knew I wasn't good at was running. As soon as I got my date for my fitness test, however, I began to train as much as I could and went for a run every night after I had put Jack to bed, still relying on my parents to mind him.

All too soon the test came about and I was wrecked after the warm up! I began to feel like I had bitten off more than I could chew but as we were led up to the starting point for the run I noticed the army men and woman waiting at the turn around point as well as at the end, to spur us on, and for me it had immediate effect.

I was only four or so minutes into the run and there were some people falling behind – I was one of them for a little bit but all of a sudden I thought about the frustrations of the last year and the reason why I was there and, within those thoughts, I found a strength I hadn't known I possessed, which enabled me to pick up pace. I wasn't going to let this beat me. I was given the opportunity of thirteen minutes that could change my life and I was going to take it.

Sweating and exhausted I passed the finish line in the middle of the bunch and with a minute left to spare. I had been running for my life and it had paid off. Afterwards the soldiers separated us into two groups – those of us that had passed our fitness test and those of us that hadn't. I was called into the victorious group and it was the most amazing feeling. I felt like I had achieved something already. I dug deep inside myself and had done it. I now knew, however, that it was a reality and I would have to leave my son to train, but I felt like if I did I could make a better life for both of us in the future and for one moment I felt like I could do anything.

The other people that had passed the fitness test that day were given a start date of just four weeks away, but the army had agreed to give me four months before I started, as I wanted to finish college before I left.

No more running away.

Chapter 17 – Jack and Danny

LIFE went back to normal for the next few weeks as I continued in college to finish out my broadcasting and arts course. My friend, Brid, and I presented a daily radio programme, *A Day in the Life,* for the college station – the format of which would see us interview a different person during a typical day in their life. The show had seen us chat to bands, professionals and even the likes of Dustin the turkey!

On one particular day we were supposed to be interviewing a fire fighter when at the last minute, just before we were leaving for the interview, the officer at the local fire station phoned and cancelled due to an emergency.

Brid and I were racing around trying to find a replacement interview with no luck when my friend Dave popped into my head. Dave was a fire fighter for the Air Corps and even though I believed it to be a long shot I said I would ring him and see if he was in work and could get permission for us to come and interview him at the station. Dave always pulled through for me and after two quick calls he said, "Yep, no probs, come on down at four o'clock, we have a good crew on today."

He really saved the day.

On the way over in the car Brid and I were joking about me looking a mess that day.

"Typical, the one day we are going to meet hunky fire fighters and I come into college looking horrible in a tracksuit, no makeup and a cap!" I laughed.

"Trust you to be worried about that, you look fine," she assured me.

"I guess it can't be helped now, have you got all of the interview questions?"

"Yep, it would be good for you to do the interview today because you know Dave so we can have a bit more fun with it," Brid suggested as we pulled up to the barracks.

"God, I cannot believe I am going to be living in a place like this soon, it is so intimidating," I gasped.

"You will be in your element when the time comes, but try not to think about that today," she said.

"I know, I must be crazy – the army? I cry if somebody shouts at me, how will I cope?! Rights let's get on with the job in hand," I swiftly changed the subject so as to save my own nerves.

"Go through those questions with me one more time."

Dave met us at the gates and we followed him around to the fire station. Having a tour wasn't something that the average person got to do so we were both excited. When we got there we immediately noticed another fireman outside, in his uniform, washing his car and I looked at Brid, who knew exactly what I was thinking, before I mumbled, "Check him out, he is a bit hot!"

Almost immediately Dave introduced us to his friend Danny and I simply couldn't take my eyes off him. This stereotypically gorgeous fireman was standing in front of us with a hose in his hand washing his car and I was just staring!

"Hi," I said shyly.

"Brill Dave, you have found some girls to help me clean my car," was the first thing Danny said to me as he pretended to hand me a sponge.

As soon as I heard him speak I was hooked. That beautiful northern accent came out and coupled with his perfect smile he seemed almost too good to be true.

"Dave mentioned to me that you guys were here to interview him about what it is like to be a fireman," the beautiful Belfast accent continued. "You see, though, what you really want to do is interview me too. I know all the inside info on this place, and on Dave too," he grinned.

So before we knew it we had two people to interview… and I certainly wasn't complaining. Dave and Dan showed us around the station, introducing us to everybody and afterwards we sat down in one of the rooms with a cup of tea to do the interview. All of a sudden I didn't know what to say. I had started this day thinking I was just going to be having a chat with my friend over a cuppa, but now that Dan was there I was feeling self-conscious. It must have been twenty takes before we got the interview done because we had to keep stopping as we were all laughing so much. I honestly couldn't remember the last time I had so much fun and Dan's joke answers began to help me to relax. We finally got sorted and afterwards Dan then suggested that he and Dave take Brid and I out for a ride on one of the fire engines.

Reaching out to take my hand, I found myself climbing into this huge red fire engine being helped by Dan and as soon as I reached the top step I was face to face with him. We had one of those moments where you knew what the other person was thinking but we didn't speak a word. I just looked into his beautiful blue eyes and he looked into mine and smiled. I smiled back and took a seat behind Dave as Dan picked up the radio inside the truck.

"Tower from rescue two. Looking for permission to proceed down camp, radio will be manned at all times!"

Now I really was hooked! That gorgeous accent from a gorgeous guy hanging on to the side of the fire truck, showing off no doubt, but so charming all the same. Dave stopped at the other end of the camp and turned to look at Brid and me, "Right who wants to come up and sit in the front? I will even let you put the lights on!"

Brid jumped at the offer so Dan hopped in beside me. Even then I couldn't stop thinking about what a nice guy he was and I was trying to force myself not to be shy. We had the best craic in the fire engine that day, not something you get to do every day, so I hated when it was eventually time to go.

I looked at Brid as Dan took my hand once again and helped me climb down from the fire truck. She already knew that I fancied him and smiled at me before whispering, "what a beautiful accent!"

I didn't want to leave. I knew I wouldn't be brave enough to ask for his number as I had been burned so badly by Adam, but I also knew I hadn't looked at anyone like that in a long time. I didn't know how to speak to men like that anymore. I was overcautious and had, over the past year, become self-conscious and shy.

"I will give you a ring soon and we will meet up.

Today was great," Dave shouted across at me as I got into my car.

Smiling I replied, "Thanks so much, both of you. You really did get us out of a mess today."

We said goodbye then and Brid and I drove the whole way home chatting about how much fun we had had that day, and about Dan.

I don't think I had ever had such an instant attraction to someone before and Brid was trying to convince me to text Dave and ask him for Danny's number, but she also knew that I was afraid of men and relationships after what happened, so she didn't push it too much.

Still debating the issue, with Brid gently reminding me that I had not stopped smiling since we left the camp and saying that she had never seen me like that before, my phone suddenly beeped. We weren't even back home by then so I waited until I pulled into my estate and stopped the car at the top of the road to read the message. It was from Dan!! I couldn't believe he was texting me and I read the message out to Brid with the biggest smile on my face, *Hey Aoife. It's Dan here. I hope you don't mind but I asked Dave for your number. I really had a great day with you guys today. I would love to see you again?*

I couldn't take my eyes off the phone. This never happened to me. I had been so guarded since becoming pregnant that meeting someone was the last thing on my mind.

We had been texting each other back forth for about twenty minutes when I suddenly realised that we had been so busy having fun that day that I had never mentioned that I had a son. Dan was a twenty-three-year-old man. Would he really be interested in dating a single mother? I loved my son more than life, but I was young and still sensitive about what people would think of me being a single mother. I was afraid of people judging me and I had also made a promise to Jack, although I knew he didn't understand me; that I would never let just any random man come in and out of his life. I know I was getting carried away with myself and this lovely guy had only just sent me a text, but I couldn't help it. I was scared.

In the middle of my rant to myself, Dan text me again, *If I asked you out on a date this weekend would you say yes?*

I really liked this guy and I wanted to go on a date with him so I decided to stop letting my mind run away with me. I was still young and it was perfectly fine to still have a life. I was the only person labelling me and that didn't make any sense. It was time to live again, so I sent him a text back.

You say a time and place and I will be there!

*

The first night we went out was one I will never forget. It was just nice and simple and he was so easy to talk to. We went for a drink and chatted for hours. He gave me butterflies and I loved being in his company. No awkward silences. It felt, very quickly, that we had known each other for ages.

And so one date turned into two and two dates into three before I realised that it really could be turning into something. I liked the way Dan made me feel about myself and he didn't let me down – unlike Adam. But I had now known Dan for three weeks and weighing heavily on my mind was the fact that I hadn't yet told him about Jack. I wanted him to get to know me for me first, but it was becoming a big issue in my head. I didn't want him to run and I was afraid.

One night Dan and I went out with Dave and a few other friends on our forth date and I promised myself beforehand that I would tell him before the night was out. We had a great time and I knew with certainty that I really had strong feelings for him. I had been trying to protect myself from getting hurt and protect Jack by not telling Dan about him, but there was nothing for it, I had to take the risk.

The logic of a young girl in her twenties doesn't always compute and I soon realised how wrong I was by not telling him straight away. I had a beautiful son who I was so proud of. What was I doing? Dan was treating me like I had never been treated by any guy before and when we were together he acted like I was the only person in the room.

He was someone special, I knew this, so I finally brought him outside of the pub for a chat.

We were in Temple bar so it was busy outside and everybody around us was having a great night. Some people had a few too many but the atmosphere was good. To begin with we were just chatting about our night, but all the time I was trying to work up the courage to say I had something to tell him. Gradually, in my mind, I started to back out, convincing myself *this*

121

is not the time or place, when my racing thoughts were interrupted by Dan.

"Wow, it is 2am already, I have been having such a good night I thought it was only about 12!"

I just nodded, but then he said something that really threw me. "I don't want this night to end, Aoife. I really like you and I'm having a great time, but I bet you will be really tired having to get up early with the baby in the morning?"

The baby? He knew I had a son? I couldn't even look at him. My eyes fell to the floor in shame. I should have been the one to say. I should have been braver, but placing his hand gently under my chin and raising my head to look into my eyes he smiled and all my fears melted away.

"I have always known babe, I knew since before I met you that day at the fire station. Dave told me before you even came over."

I couldn't believe I had worked myself up so much for something he had known all along. I couldn't believe I hadn't the courage to be honest from the start. The next words out of his mouth simply made me realise that he was slowly becoming the man of my dreams, "Did you really think that because you had a son, it was going to stop me from asking you out on a date? I knew you had been trying to tell me something for a while and I wanted to make it easy for you. It doesn't change anything and I would really love to meet your son."

I had spent so long trying to justify Adam's actions that I forgot there were still decent men out there who would like me for myself, and without a moment's hesitation I wiped the tear that had been sitting on my cheek away, and pulled Dan in close to me,

"I would really like that too."

In the weeks that followed, I fell deeper and deeper for Dan. He was the most amazing man I had ever met. He treated me with so much respect and I wanted to spend any spare time I had with him.

One morning, as the sound of my phone ringing woke me, a smile quickly spread across my face. I didn't even have to look at the screen. Dan was the first person I spoke to every day and he would ring me every morning before work.

"Morning babe, what are your plans for the day?"

Still half asleep I sat up in my bed and glanced at the clock.

"I only had one lecture in college and I guess I have just missed it. Mum took Jack out this morning and I must have fallen back asleep."

"It's well for some, will Jack be back soon? I have to go up to Newry to pick up a part for my car and I was thinking maybe you and Jack would want to come with me for the drive? If it is OK with you I would love to meet him. We can all go together and bring him to a playground when we get there?"

I loved the idea. It felt like the right time and so we made a plan.

Dan came to pick us up later and as he set up Jack's car seat in the back of the car I said, "You look like a pro, are you sure you haven't been around kids before? I still can't get that stupid car seat in right!"

"Don't speak too soon," Dan laughed. "I hate admitting defeat but how do you get this part to go through here?"

I was busy trying to push the seatbelt through when I looked around and realised that Jack had come out into the garden and introduced himself to Dan by showing him his little car. He was just going on twenty months and was full of chat. The interaction seemed to come so naturally to both of them.

I smiled to myself and got Jack ready for the journey with Dan; and it wasn't long before we were driving up the road.

On the way I asked Jack if he knew my friend's name and he answered, without batting an eyelid, "Yes, his name is Daddy".

Dan and I looked at each other and burst out laughing before I corrected him and said, "Nearly, honey, his name is Danny."

At that stage, like any child his age, he had a little trouble with some pronunciation and no matter what way he tried it always came out sounding like Daddy. Dan just smiled and said that is fine with him, so I joked that maybe Jack was trying to tell me something.

Dan was quickly becoming a very important person in my life and the first day he spent with *the* most important person in my life was a special one. They just clicked and all Jack wanted was to sit beside Dan and hold his hand all day.

We enjoyed the next few months together. A lot of our dates ended up in parks feeding the ducks with Jack or at the zoo or the pet farm. Dan saw Jack and me as a team, a package deal, and he just fitted in with us naturally. Most of our day trips were his idea and heading up to the north became a common Saturday day out too. I was so nervous the first time Dan brought Jack and me up to meet his family in Belfast.

I knew they had heard a lot about me, but the fears of the past and people judging me began to slip back into my mind. I freely admit I can be my own worst enemy and I couldn't help but wonder would they really want their young son dating a girl with a child? I soon realised how wrong I was to worry when Dan's parents welcomed both Jack and I into their home with open arms. They had even phoned Dan the day before and found out what Jack's favourite food was so they could have it waiting for him before we arrived. I never thought I would be able to let my guard down again, after what had happened in the past, but that is exactly what it was, the past. And

Jack, Dan and I together just felt right.
Together, we felt like the future.

Chapter 18 – I nearly lost it all!

I KNEW in the back of my mind that the clock was ticking and I would soon be going away to train with the army, but I was still determined that no matter who came along I would find a way to support my son – I wasn't letting myself rely on anybody else. Even the man I was falling in love with.

During my first few months with Dan, I had received my notification from the army telling me I had to report to Aiken barracks, in Dundalk, to begin my training. This was where I would be based during my first few months from the 30th of May. I was very excited, but I was gutted at the same time. I had been so focused on the army until Dan came along, but now I had this wonderful boyfriend and I wanted to spend all of my free time with him, yet still I had to leave. I didn't know if we had been together long enough to survive a long distance relationship, because I knew that during my training I would only be allowed to leave the barracks at the weekend, and even at that not every weekend. There would be some weekends when we wouldn't be allowed to leave at all and the recruits that had children would only be allowed to have their children brought up to the barracks to see them for two hours on a Sunday. *What was I doing? How could I spend that much time away from my son? How could I risk losing my boyfriend for a job?* I was so temped to leave things as they were and not go to the army, but then I reminded myself, *who knows what the future holds? What if my relationship doesn't work out and I find myself back where I started?*

I needed to do this. I needed to be independent for myself and for my son.

No more running away.

My new motto in life.

Dan and I had loads of conversations about when I was to leave and, eventually, we worked out a plan that we felt could make it work. We could spend weekends together and speak on the phone every day. Then on the weekends that I wasn't allowed to leave the barracks, Dan said he would collect Jack in my mum and dad's house and bring him up to see me. He really was an amazing man – one in a million – and I believed that as long as we stayed considerate of each other we could do this.

All too soon the day came when I had to say goodbye to my son. I can't even write about that day now without crying so I really don't understand how I walked out that door. He didn't understand that mummy was going to try and create a future for him, and it broke my heart. But in order to remain strong and resolute I reminded myself of how far from being that lost little girl I had come, and that it was my responsibility to give my son a good role model. So with tears in my eyes I said goodbye and asked my mum to distract him in the back garden so he wouldn't see me leave. Dan was there to bring me up to Dundalk and held me tight before we drove away, as I fought to overcome the emotion of leaving my son. We drove up the motorway in silence at first. It was a beautiful day, but I felt a huge cloud over me the further away from my son we got.

Dan, even though he didn't want me to leave, always put my needs and feelings before his own so it wasn't long before he started trying to cheer me up.

"Come on babe, you will be fine. You know you can do this and you know you will get home this weekend and I will be waiting for you. It is really only four days away."

I knew he didn't believe it was going to be easy but I also knew he would do anything to make me happy, even if that meant hiding his own heartache from me. I could see it in his eyes though. The phrase *if you love someone, let them go...* comes to mind and I have no doubt that Dan was struggling with driving me away from our life together, as much as I was. I wouldn't have got through that day without him.

We were at least halfway to Dundalk by the time I stopped crying.

"Babe," he continued. "I am so proud of you and I know Jack will be too. I am going to give your mum a ring during the week and organise to collect Jack on Wednesday from the crèche and bring him to dinner. I can fill you in then on how he is getting on and I won't have to wait a week to see him. I can be his connection to you."

Not only was this amazing man supporting me through moving away, but he was supporting my little boy missing his mummy too. We arrived up outside the barracks and I didn't know if I could get out of the car. I was a mess and just sat there looking at Dan. He had been the strong one right up until we arrived at the gates of the barracks and I had never seen him cry before, but as we sat there at the side of the road the tears streamed down his face. I knew we had something special together I just hoped I was making the right decision and we would get through this.

"I don't want you to go," he finally admitted.

He had wanted to say those words to me from the start, but he put my feelings first and it was only then, when he was faced with me walking away that he felt he no longer had anything to lose.

"Promise me we won't change, Aoife. I hope you know by now that I love you."

"I love you too," I replied with my voice and heart both breaking.

"We just need to get through this week. Remember it is only four days this time. Sure that will fly."

I knew he was trying to convince himself as much as me.

Eventually it was time for me to go.

"I will be right here waiting for you on Friday, babe."

Dan then kissed my head and before I started crying again I got out of the car, just as the sun hid behind the clouds and it started to rain. Trying to lighten the mood I swung my bag over my shoulder and joked, "I hope that isn't a bad sign! You go on, love, I will be fine," and I watched him drive away.

Bag in hand I walked through those gates wiping away my tears and talking myself into being strong.

On entering I was led into a waiting room with all of the other new recruits, where we were to be assigned our uniforms and our rooms. One by one the room began to empty until there was only twenty or so of us left. My name was finally called out along with three other girls and we were led to the stores where we got fitted for our uniforms and shown to our room on the female lines. When we got there I sat on my bed and wondered how I was going to stick it. The other girls in the room were lovely though, so supportive when they heard I had left a son at home, and it wasn't long before they had me focused again and actually excited about the new journey we were about to embark on together.

I don't know how or why it happened, I think maybe it was a self-preservation method, a way of getting myself through the thoughts that were too hard on my emotions, like leaving my son and Dan; but something in me changed that very first day. I became almost too focused and in doing so distanced myself from anything other than the army. I wasn't allowing myself to think about life outside those gates and I quickly fitted into the army way of life. I would call Dan every evening or he would call me, but he quickly noticed the change in me when all I had to talk about was the army. I had become cold to anything else. What made it worse was that I didn't even see it. I was running away again, running away from reality. Still, just like he promised, Dan was there waiting for me at the gates on my first weekend home and I was so happy to see him. He drove me straight to see Jack and he spent the evening with us.

We weren't long at home, however, when my phone started to beep with messages from all my new friends at the barracks. I must have spent most of that weekend on the phone, buzzing from all of the new experiences while poor Dan persevered. Something had definitely changed. I was blocking everything out.

Sunday came quickly and it was time for me to leave. Once again Dan drove me back up the road to the barracks, but this time there weren't any tears. He was his normal loving self but would later tell me that he was just hoping the real Aoife would resurface when I settled in.

Over the next couple of months though, instead of things getting better and more settled in our relationship, our new circumstances saw things getting worse and worse. If it wasn't army related I was out.

I didn't recognise myself, but kept my head down and kept going. Whenever Dan was telling me I was distant or that I had to remember that there was life outside those big gates, I just fobbed him off and told him, and myself, that this way of life wasn't forever and I was getting closer and closer to coming home.

But in reality, I was pushing home and everything that it stood for, further and further away.

Then the day came that would shock me into change…

It was the weekend and the army weren't allowing us out because we had a night shoot on the range, so any recruits with children were told that they could invite their kids up for two hours on Sunday. Dan was so happy to hear this as he had thought we wouldn't get to see each other that weekend. So he collected Jack and headed up the motorway to me. I was excited to see them both. When Dan got to me I was told I could bring my son into the town for the two hours. The other recruits were disappointed that they would not get out so a few of them asked me to pick them up some bits and bobs from the shop. I didn't think much of it and brought my list of shopping to the car to meet Dan and Jack. My two boys were so happy to see me and as we drove towards the town I asked Dan to stop at the shopping centre so I could pick up some bits for the girls stuck in the barracks.

I then went on to spend the only two hours I had for two weeks with my son and my boyfriend shopping for other people and talking about the army. I didn't take my son to the playground or my loving, amazing, boyfriend to lunch. I didn't spend time asking him how he was or if he had any news from home. I spent my only two hours thinking of the army. I knew at the time it wasn't the right thing to do, but I wouldn't allow myself to let anything else in.

What was I doing to my family – to myself?

I had changed and not in a good way, in the worst possible way.

I knew by the time Dan dropped me off that he was upset, but I acted as if everything was OK, gave my boys a kiss and got out of the car. Something didn't feel right to me saying goodbye to them that day though. Still, as had become the norm, I pushed it to the back of my mind and walked back through the gates that would allow me return to my life on the other side. The army, somewhere along the line, had become my support structure.

They understood what I was trying to do.

That Friday we had to do a route march and I always dreaded them. I wasn't very good at them and the corporals never made it easy. There was also usually a mountain we had to climb while carrying our full kit on our backs. It was on that march that it first hit home how much of a family our platoon had become and how we had earned the right to be a part of that family just by wearing the uniform. Nothing else was needed and I felt accepted. It was the first time since I had Jack that those barriers came down and I allowed other people, outside my family, to support me when I needed it. Before then I had been so focused on "staying strong" and "doing it on my own," but on that particular day I couldn't find the strength. We were knee-deep in mud and I kept getting my boots stuck. I had zero energy left, but the whole way through my platoon sergeant kept shouting back to anybody behind him, "Anyone who doesn't finish this route march will not be getting home this weekend."

I had to find the strength to get home to my boys, I just had to, but after one last push and a hundred more metres my body gave up on me and I felt defeated. It was so much more than a route march to me. Each step was a step closer to freedom for the weekend, a step closer to my son, so sitting there on a rock, head to toe in mud and my rifle across my knees, a wave of self pity came over me. I wasn't strong enough.

I had nothing left physically or mentally. Exhausted, one of the girls and one of the guys from my section approached me.

"No one gets left behind," they shouted.

I hadn't got the energy left to do it on my own so I reached out to grab an outstretched hand and followed as this girl pulled me the rest of the way up the mountain while the other recruit stayed behind me, with his hands on my back, urging me forward. Both had their own kit and rifle to carry yet they still reached out to me, helping me regain my strength, and when we reached the last hundred metres of the track they let go; but ran right by my side so I could feel the same sense of achievement that they did as we crossed the finish line together.

*

The next evening was spent in my room with the girls as we had a big inspection to prepare for so we were all working hard polishing our boots and ironing our uniforms. If there was a crease to be found, the corporals training us would find it, so this process took hours. It was during my attempt to put a shine in my boots that my phone rang.

It was Dan.

I made my way to the step in the courtyard, where I would regularly go to find some privacy to speak when he called, and almost immediately I knew that something was wrong.

"Hi, babe, the girls and I are trying to get ready for an inspection, it takes ages. You got home OK yesterday?"

"Yeah, fine."

The hairs on the back on my neck stood up immediately. I had never heard him with this tone before so I felt compelled to ask.

"What's wrong? You don't sound like yourself?"

I really didn't want to hear the answer.

"We need to talk," was all he said. Never a good sign, and within a few seconds his words broke my heart.

"Aoife, I can't do this anymore. I can't stand back and watch what you are doing to yourself and how much you are changing. I don't know you anymore. I know I should always come behind your son in your priorities, but how can you justify both your son and me playing second fiddle to a job? You don't need me anymore, you don't even talk to me anymore, not properly. You get all you need from your new army friends and I am just left on the sideline. You won't let me in."

I had been so busy in army mode that I hadn't been hearing anything else from the outside world – but I heard this loud and clear. His voice was cracking up on the other end of the phone and I knew he was crying as he said the words, "I can't put myself through it anymore. Every time I drop you at the gates I know I will get a little bit less of you back when I see you again and it has got to the stage where I don't know you anymore. Aoife, it is breaking my heart to say this, but you are not the girl I fell in love with."

It hurt like nothing had ever hurt before.

I had pushed the man I loved so much, so far away from me that he felt he couldn't stay with me, but all I could say in that moment was, "Please don't do this."

"Babe, we had something so special in each other, but it's not me, it's you throwing it away for a job. No job is worth that."

I began to cry for the first time since I got there, which was pretty significant given that I'm an emotional person, I cry all the time – even at the news – so this was a real release and I realised then that I had become cold. I wasn't me anymore.

"Dan, you know I am doing this for my son."

I was desperately trying to justify my actions, not just to him, but to myself.

"I have to make him proud of me," I whispered, as other soldiers walked through the courtyard, looking at me sitting down in the corner.

"When are you going to see, Aoife? When are you going to understand that Jack doesn't care what job you do? Jack will be proud of you whatever you do, whether you're a stay-at-home mummy or work in a shop or an office. Jack will be proud of you for being you and being with him. He needs you there to play with him and read him stories and put him to bed and tuck him in. He doesn't need this."

I felt like I had been hit in the heart, a pain like never before. I had been so obsessed with making him proud that I had actually let him down. I had let Dan down too and like a light switch being flicked, it was suddenly clear as day.

But it was also too late.

"Babe, please don't do this. I know it was me throwing us away but I can see that now. I need you to hold on. Don't leave and I will show you, I promise."

I knew I was asking too much but I still hoped. I couldn't lose him. Not now.

"I need some time," he finally answered. "You know I have always been honest with you, I hate games and I don't know if I can trust you again. Aoife, if we are not going to be stable I have to walk away. It isn't fair on anyone, especially Jack."

Jack, my beautiful baby boy. He wasn't even old enough to understand where mummy had gone and I had made such a mess of everything. Now here was a man, who wasn't even his father, putting him first – which was more than I was doing.

I didn't sleep a wink that night in the barracks and as soon as the hustle and bustle of a Monday morning began I requested a meeting with the officer looking after our platoon. I stood to attention in his office and told him, with no uncertainty, that it was time for me to leave.

The army is an amazing way of life and it had taught me a lot, but it wasn't going to be my way of life. I knew that now. I am very proud of the sacrifices our soldiers make for our country, but they came at too big a cost for me and it was time for me to go home. It took a couple of days to organise, but I got to work straight away at packing away what had become my life in order to try and save the life that I really wanted. I told Dan what I had done and I hoped he would still be there, but resolute, he said that he needed some time to think things over and that he wouldn't be there on the Wednesday when I was coming home for good. He was going away for a few days to get things clear in his head and he would phone me in a couple of days.

I prayed I hadn't done too much damage to us and hoped against hope that it wasn't too late. I had found the man of my dreams and I was so disappointed in myself that I had let him slip away.

I spent the next few days doing lovely things with my son while waiting for Dan to call me, and when he eventually did I hadn't got a clue what to say. He told me that I had hurt him a lot, but a life without me would hurt him more and he trusted what I was telling him when I said that I wanted to try again. He did too.

"This is it though, Aoife. You and me, we can't mess this up again. This has to be us," he said as relief washed over me.

I just couldn't believe, after everything I had put him through, that he was still there. It was then that I realised the extent of my love for him and I couldn't have been happier.

Our future was finally set. It was Dan, Jack and I and we were going to make it work.

I was going to make it work.

Chapter 19 – Dreams do come true

JUST like that, I was me again. I had taken a major wrong turn in my life, but Dan came to the rescue. He had taught me, for the first time, what it meant to be a proper mummy. It was ironic, after all my efforts, that he had ended up being a daddy to Jack before I had learned how to be a mummy, and it was this bond that was turning us into a proper family.

I aspired to be like him and things got better day after day. We were connected again and I was happier than I had ever thought possible.

Our trips to Belfast became a common occurrence again and Dan's family were slowly becoming an extension of our own. Jack would regularly wait for Dan's car to pull into the driveway and he would race out to give his "Daddy Danny" a hug.

"Can we go to Belfast today? I want to go to Belfast," Jack would scream with excitement.

"I want to see Nanny Maura and Papa Danny! Please please please."

Dan's dad had gotten into a routine whenever we went up there and he would meet us at the car when we pulled up.

"Right, Jack, are you ready? Me and you are going to go for a walk," he would say, and away they would trot, hand in hand – Jack and his honorary grandpa.

It happened so naturally, becoming a family. I often marvelled, from that point, at the amount of time I had wasted worrying about Jack and his need for a father – his father – because I had finally realised that Jack didn't need a father, any man can be a father, he needed a daddy. And now he had one. The best one we could have wished for and the best second nanny and papa too.

Those few months were amazing as Danny gave me the security that I had yearned for, for so long. He constantly told me, "As long as you are you, I'm there and I always will be." And so I was determined never to change again.

I began to enjoy life again and living without the pressure of trying to do something big so Jack would be proud of me, was priceless. I knew by being a good mummy, Jack would be happy and that is all we needed. I got myself a part-time job in a veterinary surgery so I could work half days and spend more time with him. Life was good, things with Dan were better than ever, and before I knew it, it was the week of our first anniversary. We had come so close to not making it, but we learned from all that had happened and took strength from that.

When the day came Dan told me he had planned a nice time for us, and so I asked mum and dad if they would mind Jack for me after work. It was a cold day in March and he picked me up and took me on a drive up the Wicklow Mountains. The higher we climbed the foggier it got, but that just added to the romantic nature of the day and I was happy just to be with him.

"There is a lovely little pub in Wicklow that we can go to for lunch," he said.

"You have done your research I see, I am impressed," I replied with a grin.

It was a beautiful drive and although it wasn't raining the fog was getting thick.

"Look, Dan, there is Powerscourt waterfall," I said excitedly. "We have to get out so I can show you this."

It was beautiful and there was a viewpoint there so we decided to go for a walk and get a closer look at the falls from the top. We walked through a field and right up to the edge of the waterfall, where our breath was immediately stolen away. It was stunning.

"Are you cold babe?" he asked, as he wrapped his coat around me.

"I seriously can't believe it has been a year, and after everything I have put you through you are still here," I mused.

"Stop beating yourself up about that already! We all make mistakes and if we didn't make mistakes then what would we ever learn from? All I care about is that we are here and I have never been this happy."

"You are a wise man, Mr Curran and, lucky for me, a patient one too."

"Are you happy Aoife? Am I really enough to make you happy?" he asked then.

I smiled. "I didn't know that this type of happiness existed. You have turned me into the best possible version of myself and you are everything to me."

It was so true. Dan had shown me a whole new world and I felt like I was on top of it, standing over this waterfall, watching the fog roll over the edge with the water. He gave me a hug then that seemed to last a lifetime and suddenly, out of nowhere it seemed, he reached into his pocket before getting down on one knee.

The world stopped turning that very second, and my heart stopped beating.

This couldn't be happening, really?

But it was and Dan was smiling at me with that gorgeous face and saying, "Aoife will you marry me? I want you to become my wife, I want Jack to be my son."

I couldn't even give him an answer. I just burst into tears and grabbed hold of him.

"Can I assume that is a yes then?" He asked, laughing.

"Yes!" I shouted from the top of my lungs, as I thought I was going to burst with happiness.

My face hurt from smiling and I couldn't take my eyes off my gorgeous fiancé as he placed a beautiful diamond ring on my finger. Then we walked hand in hand down the waterfall edge. Bliss.

It was only when we got back to the car and had calmed down a bit that Dan realised he had knelt down in sheep poo when he proposed, so we had a good laugh about that!

I couldn't wait to tell everyone but with no reception where we were I had to wait to get to the pub for lunch before phoning our families to tell them the good news. Everyone was over the moon for us and couldn't wait to hear how Dan had proposed. What an amazing day! It had been perfect. We drove back to my house later and I couldn't wait to see Jack, because here we were creating a family for him, a proper family.

When we got there mum and dad were waiting at the front door to congratulate us. Turns out they had known a lot longer than me, because Dan had taken the time, the week before, to go and speak to them and ask them for my hand in marriage.

So they had the champagne in the fridge waiting for us and we sat for a while, sipping it and talking over all of the excitement.

Suddenly Dan asked me if I was ready to go.

"Go? Where are we going?"

He had it all organised with my parents to mind Jack for the night and was whisking me away to a beautiful hotel. I was overwhelmed. It didn't feel that long ago that I had been scared and alone, yet here I was engaged to the man of my dreams with a beautiful son and the greatest families surrounding us.

Dan and I spent that night talking all about our future together, where we would live and our wedding plans. I had to pinch myself. I couldn't wait to travel up to Belfast to show his family the ring and talk about everything.

The day we did they were as amazing as ever.

Full of congratulations the first thing Dan's mum said to me was one of the kindest comments I had ever been on the receiving end of.

"Wedding or not, you are a part of our family and Jack will always be our first grandson." My happiness was complete. They had taken my baby into their hearts and accepted him as one of their own right from the start. It's not every day that you come across so many people, from the same family, all with the kindest and most welcoming of attitudes. Now those people were our family too and I was immensely proud.

*

Everybody wanted to help us with the wedding plans and we soon set the date and got busy with all of the preparations. It was that year that Dan and I also bought our first house together in Kildare, so money was tight anyway, nevermind planning a wedding on top it all! But I couldn't wait to get married and I had help wherever I turned, whether it was in Dublin with mum helping me with the venue and my dress or in Belfast, with Dan's parents helping me with the bridesmaid's dresses, the decorations and our honeymoon. I was on top of the world and if it wasn't for my parents and Dan's parents we would never have had the wedding we did.

Before we knew it Dan and I were just weeks away from getting married and the excitement was in full swing. Dress fittings and hotel meetings, there was always something to do. There was, however, one other important thing that Dan and I had been talking about – and it had nothing to do with the wedding.

Dan was already Jack's daddy, his father and his best friend, but it was time for us to go back down that road and make it all official.

Adoption, here we go again!

Dan, and I, wanted him to adopt Jack, so we could all come full circle as a family. It was so important to us, so we began to look into the process, but as I knew only too well when it came to adoption, time and patience was the key and we were told that we weren't allowed to even start applying until we got married. Adoption law in Ireland is so strict and outdated at times, so much so that the adoption board said they would not even give us an application *form* until we produced a marriage certificate.

This frustrated us both as with Dan already being Jack's daddy we didn't feel like we needed a certificate to prove that, but with Jack starting school the following year we wanted him to be a Curran in time for September. If he wasn't it would lead to him having to change his name after he started, which in turn would have caused confusion with everybody.

We knew at this stage that the adoption process would probably take at least eighteen months, so the most immediate solution was to change Jack's surname by deed poll. The process was simple enough and all we had to do was sign an affidavit in the presence of a solicitor, stating our reasons for it and the circumstances surrounding the change.

Normally I would have had to get the "father's" consent for a change like this, but I explained in the deed poll that it had just been Jack and I from the start and he hadn't had any involvement.

Our deed poll went before a review board in the high court, which felt I was justified in making this decision and the confirmation came through a couple of weeks before our wedding. As a result Jack became a Curran before I did!

Everything was falling into place. We had spoken about children a lot in that year and Dan and I both wanted to add to our family as soon as possible, but we didn't want Jack to feel any different from any other member of the family, so we were always mindful of him within our plans.

The wedding day came in a flash and it was a real fairy tale event. When I woke up that morning I wasn't nervous at all. I just could not wait to walk up the aisle to my soon-to-be husband. I had stayed in my parents' house the night before and Dan and Jack had stayed at our house with a few of his friends and my brother. The morning was great fun, getting ready with my bridesmaids, Clare, Katherine and Amy, who all made sure that everything was organised and ready to go. And before I knew it, I was in the wedding car with my dad and on our way to meet my prince. There we had a lovely few minutes of calm, just for us, and having had hardly any chance to talk to dad beforehand, I relished them.

We arrived at the church (a little late) and I stood there, feeling like the luckiest woman in the world, waiting to walk up the aisle to the man of my dreams. I was surprisingly calm as the doors finally opened and one by one my bridesmaids left my side and began the long walk to the top of the church.

Finally it was just my dad and me and I linked his arm as he took my hand.

I looked at him and he simply nodded with a smile. I could see if he spoke he would not be able to hold it together, so I just squeezed his hand and we began our walk towards the rest of my life.

The first face I saw smiling down at me was my beautiful handsome son. As we got closer to Father Kevin, the same family friend that had christened Jack, he put his hand on Dan's shoulder and smiled at him. It was only the second time in my life I cried from pure joy, the first was the first day I laid eyes on my baby, and I wiped a single tear away from my cheek before smiling at my boys.

During the service Mary did a reading and it wasn't until that moment that I made sense of the second chance Dan had given me all those months ago.

"Love is patient, love is kind. It is not jealous, (love) is not pompous, it is not inflated, it is not rude, it does not seek its own interests, it is not quick tempered, it does not brood over injury, and it does not rejoice over wrongdoing but rejoices with the truth. It bares all things, believes all things hopes all things, and endures all things. Love never fails. If there are prophecies, they will be brought to nothing; if tongues, they will cease; if knowledge, it will be brought to nothing. For we know partially and we prophesy partially, but when perfect comes, the partial will pass away. When I was a child, I used to talk as

a child, think as a child, reason as a child; when I became a man, I put aside my childish things. For now we see through a glass darkly; but then face to face.

At present I know partially; then I shall know fully, as I am fully known. So faith, hope, love remain, these three; but the greatest of these is love."

Those beautiful words were so simple, yet meant so much, and I knew then that it was no coincidence I had come to that day.

Love endures all things and rejoices with the truth.

I looked at my Dan. I knew how much his love had endured to get us to that point and I would never forget those words.

It was a magical day from start to finish and we had the time of our lives. We were a family and I was now Mrs Curran – a name I carried, and still do, with pride. We enjoyed every second, but the rest of the day passed in a flash. I remember, at one point, looking around the packed ballroom, where all our friends and family were celebrating with us, and wishing I could freeze time. It was just so overwhelming to see how far we had come. All of my families were in the same room, together. Mum and dad and all of my relatives, Dan's family, Mary, Mick and all of Mary's family – all smiling, laughing and sharing this time together. It was more than special.

We had organised to go, straight away, on our honeymoon to the west coast of America and we flew into San Francisco before hiring a convertible to drive to LA, spend five days there and then drive on down to Las Vegas. Mum, dad and Dan's parents had all offered to look after Jack between them, while we were gone for two weeks, and after all of the months of planning we couldn't wait for our trip of a lifetime.

We were so tired by the time we got to San Francisco that we spent our time there relaxing, taking in the sights; and we had only just recovered when it was time for our road trip to Los Angles. We travelled down the coast enjoying the most amazing scenery and sights, chatting away like we hadn't a care in the world. We were simply full of excitement about our future together and all of the plans we had – including Jack's adoption. The one phone call I made after the wedding, before we left for our honeymoon, was to the adoption board requesting an application from, so we knew that would be waiting for us when we returned home.

We arrived to the paradise that is Los Angeles and checked into our hotel in Santa Monica, full of beans. This really was the trip of a lifetime and I was getting to do it with my best friend and the love of my life. Later that first day we sat by the pool overlooking the beach and in our relaxed state I decided that it was time I told Dan something I had been wondering about for a few days.

Obviously we had spoken about wanting a bigger family, but for some reason I was afraid to say out loud what I needed to.

"I don't think life could get much better than this, look at this view," Dan said as he took my hand and pulled me over to sit with him.

"I think I am pregnant Dan," I blurted out, afraid to look at his face as my mind flashed back to the first time I had ever said those words, and the reaction I got from the father.

I guess somewhere inside I still carried the scars.

I was only a couple of seconds, with these thoughts racing through my head, however, before I finally looked at Dan who, like a kid at Christmas, had the biggest smile on his face. It was like he didn't know what to say or do so he jumped up and took my hand, tears filling his eyes, and said, "We have to go and find a pharmacy right now! How amazing would it be if you were?!"

Over and over again this amazing man was showing me what it felt like to have somebody really love you. So we got the tests and raced back to the hotel room where, one by one, I began to take them; and one by one I saw those familiar blue lines. Impatiently waiting outside the door I could hear Dan pacing the floor, so eventually I opened it to put him out of his misery.

"Well?" he asked, still pacing.

"Babe, I am pregnant!"

"Tell me you're serious? Aoife please don't be joking. You're pregnant? We are going to have a baby?"

I fell into his arms as my emotions got the better of me.

"We are going to have a baby, Jack is going to be a big brother!"

How my life had changed since the last time those two little blue lines had turned my world upside down. Jack had turned out to be the best thing that had ever happened to me, despite how scared I was at the time, and now here I was, married, happier than ever and in a beautiful hotel in Santa Monica learning that I was going to become a mummy for the second time. Dan always has a beautiful smile on his face, but I saw him smile that day like never before, after hearing he would, again, become a daddy.

There are no words to describe how much joy we felt and all of my fears melted away as I sat on the side of the bed listening to Dan who, after some pondering, said, "Do you know what I am looking forward to most babe, about the pregnancy part I mean?"

"I don't think you have got a clue what you are letting yourself in for," I joked. "I wasn't a barrel of laughs the last time, have I ever told you that?"

"That is the point," he gushed. "That is what I am looking forward to, – giving you a whole new experience to the one you had the last time around, when you were alone and pregnant. This time I will be there for it all, the morning sickness, and the doctor's appointments. Everything. I will always be holding your hand and you are going to love every minute of it. I will see to that."

Everyone was so happy to hear our news when we returned home. Especially Jack. He could not wait to have a little brother or sister to spoil. And as we expected, our letter from the adoption board was there for us to fill out and return; so we had a lot to keep us going.

The board needed to know a lot about all aspects of our life and we knew that even after we had sent the application off it would be months before we got to the top of the queue and had the social worker appointment.

But, right then, we had all the time in the world.

Chapter 20 – Adoption again

THE months before Jessica was born were filled with excitement and doctor's appointments. Dan kept his promise and it was, indeed, a whole other experience going through a pregnancy with that constant loving support; and before we knew it, I was nine months pregnant.

Again the doctors, as they had with Jack, had to induce me because of my blood pressure and after a painful, but memorable, labour, our baby daughter was born. It was June 8th, 2008, and she weighed in at a healthy 8 pounds 8 ounces. She had a beautiful big mop of black hair and was the image of her daddy. I could have watched him for hours as he whispered, "So you are what perfection looks like! I am your daddy princess and I am always going to be here to mind and protect you."

He then gently kissed me on the head and placed our new baby daughter in my arms.

"I am so proud of you babe, you have done amazingly well and look at how beautiful she is!" He was in awe.

"So you are the one that has been kicking me," I laughed as I cuddled her. "Welcome to the world darling. Your big brother can't wait to meet you."

The first call we made was to my dad's mobile, as Jack had been with my parents for the day. The moment he answered I asked dad to put him on the phone so Jack could be the first person we told about his baby sister. Mum and dad then brought him to the hospital straight away and he was over the moon to learn that the baby had brought a present for him too.

"Can I give her a kiss Mummy?" he kept asking. Then, "Daddy I am going to help mummy every day with my new sister."

And finally, "How did they get Jessica out of mummy's tummy dad?"
Suddenly it was time to go and as Dan avoided the question, he looked back at me with an awkward smile and I said, "I'll leave that one up to you babe, I have to stay here and feed Jess."

I laughed as the door swung closed behind them.

*

Within a couple of weeks we couldn't remember what life was like before we had Jessie. Every time I was up for a night feed Dan was up just to give her cuddles. We were a team and seeing how he looked after his new daughter, and still played all day with Jack too, melted my heart. The postman had been busy visiting our house those few weeks, as we received so many beautiful cards congratulating us on Jessie's arrival, when one day there was an official letter in the middle of the bunch. It was from the adoption board informing us that a social worker had been assigned to our case and she would like to organise a meeting with us at our home the following week. She requested that it only be Dan and I at the house that day, so she could explain the process to us. It also said that she would meet Jack at a later date.

Full of nervous energy, I think I cleaned the house for two full days before that first meeting and it felt like no time before the doorbell rang and a small stout lady, with short brown hair, stood on our doorstep with a big folder under her arm.

"Hello, you must be Aoife, I am Mag."

We went into the living room and Dan made everybody tea.

"It is better to do these things in person I think, so we can all get to know each other a little and I can take you through what happens next," Mag started.

She had a lovely way of relaxing us and it wasn't long before she opened the big folder she had been carrying and began to go through all of the forms that would be required for the application, including character references, Garda checks and a million and one questions. These people needed to know every detail of every aspect of our lives – this was going to be a long road.

"Don't let all these forms phase you, sure you won't?" Mag said. "If you have any problems at all just let me know and we can tackle them together. I do need to know a little bit about you today though, Aoife. Can you tell me about the time when Jack was born and what involvement the father had in his life?" She paused for a second while checking her file. "Adam isn't it?"

It was hard to revisit some of the things that the social worker wanted to, but she made me feel so comfortable just sitting there sipping her tea, that I began, for the first time in a long time, to revisit my past.

"Unfortunately as much as I wanted him to, Adam never really had much of an involvement in Jack's life," I began. "The relationship wasn't a very stable one and Adam didn't feel ready to be a father, so it was pretty much Jack and I until we met Dan," I said glancing at my loving husband with a smile.

There were tears as I relived difficult specifics and I hated the thought of needing Adam for anything. I had (in hindsight, naively so) thought that we wouldn't need his involvement. Jack was now nearly six years old and he hadn't ever been involved, and besides we had been allowed to change Jack's name without his involvement, so I was hoping this would be the same. It had been years since we had contact and to be honest I didn't even have a

142

clue how to track him down. I explained all this to the social worker and she placed her tea down on the coffee table in front of her.

"I know you are not the first girl to find yourself in a situation like this one, dear, and I am most certain that you will not be the last, but unfortunately there is no way around this part of the process. You have to consider the best possible outcome for the child and for his case we can't leave any chapter unfinished, any stone unturned. Once we find an address for Adam, we will have to inform him of your intentions for Jack, through registered post, in case he wants to contest the order."

I was terrified at the thought of opening up old wounds again so I protested slightly by asking, "Even though his name is not on the birth cert?"

"Even though his name is not on the birth cert," Mag replied.

I was dreading the thought of contacting him again, but this was not for me, it was for Jack, so I knew I had to put my feelings aside and do the right thing. My son was always the most important thing and I wouldn't leave any gaps, any unknowns, if I could help it. It is not always easy to do the right thing, but if my parents could do it for me I could do it for Jack.

Mag sat forward in her chair, lifted her head from her notes and said, "Have you informed Jack about your situation? I realise Daniel would have been the main father figure for as long as Jack could remember but have you spoken to him about this?"

As I said, honesty has always been so important to me and I had learned through my adoption story about how important it was for Jack to know as much as I had control over, but Dan stepped in and answered Mag's question.

"Jack has always known that his mummy and him didn't know me when he was born. He knew that he and Aoife had met me together and how special he was, because I fell in love with them both and wanted to be his daddy."

"That is great Daniel and it is a lovely way to put it. We would be very interested in making sure the children involved in adoptions are fully aware of the circumstances."

As kids do, Jack accepted our situation as the norm and I even had to remind him every now and again when he would ask questions like, "Do you think I look like my daddy?" or said, "Tell me about when I was born?" But just as it was with me growing up, it was talked about with ease in our house.

Mag turned to me, "Is Jack aware of his birth father?"

That was a question I didn't know how to answer. How would I approach that with him? He wasn't old enough to know about the birds and the bees and he hadn't yet realised that there are always two people involved when it comes to babies, so if his daddy wasn't there when he was born, who was? I hadn't a clue how to deal with it, as I didn't want to upset him in any way.

"I still haven't figured out how to approach that one to be honest," I said.

"That is OK, we don't expect you to have all the answers. We would, however, expect you to have spoken to him about it before we come to the end of this adoption process, but if you need any help with broaching the subject just give me a shout."

I was relieved Mag was so understanding.

"Kids are so accepting at this age, have a read though this leaflet and it might help," she continued. "Take your time and tell him when you feel it is right. Then when I come back I can speak to him if he has any questions."

It really was very helpful sitting down with Mag. We now knew what we had to prepare ourselves for on the road ahead and, more importantly, it compounded the fact that we wanted this more than anything. So we got busy with requesting Garda checks, filling out forms and figuring out how we would get contact details for Adam.

I was so nervous about opening the door to my past again and to make things worse I hadn't got a clue about how to go about it. Where would I send a letter? If I gave the adoption agency the last known address I had for him, his mother might open the letter and he mightn't react well to the secret, which he had decided to keep for all those years, being exposed. I just wanted to move on with my life and no matter what decisions he had taken in his, or what road he had decided to follow, I got through without him – so I didn't want to cause any unnecessary trouble for him now.

Who knows why he did what he did, but I had come through it OK and had no right to judge him. For the first time ever, I thought about him with compassion and empathy and I felt sorry for him, because he thought he had no other option but to walk away from his son.

Dan and I spoke at length about what the best way to contact him would be and in the end we decided that I would try and get his number from some friends who we both knew at the time. It wasn't that hard to be honest. His number hadn't changed, but when it came down to dialling it I found myself unable to pick up the phone. The last time I spoke to this man I was a different person. He was young, naive and immature too. I knew I had changed, but had he?

I had to remind myself that this wasn't an option and, besides, it was the right thing to do for our son. It would be the end of an important chapter in all our lives as well as closure for everybody, including him, and I needed to make that happen. I decided to speak to my friend who had known him at the time, to get her opinion on how to handle making contact, and after a very long conversation I had talked myself out of being the one to pick up the phone. I was fighting with myself because I knew I didn't owe Adam much, but I owed him this.

I just couldn't bring myself to do it, to feel vulnerable again, so my friend, Ciara, offered to phone him for me, after reminding me of everything I had come through without him. She said that a lot of people wouldn't even consider making that call; they would just let the adoption agency send the letter.

In the end I agreed to let her do it. I knew she would explain to him that I wasn't sending a message by not making the call myself, nor did I have any bad feelings towards him. I just wanted to get on with my life, with my son, my husband and my new baby daughter; and opening up those doors to the past would simply be too painful for everybody involved. She explained to him about our adoption plans and that I just wanted him to be aware that he would receive a letter, so it would not be a shock to him. She then asked him where he would like it to be sent.

She said he was polite enough to her on the phone, but kept on questioning why it wasn't me making the call, telling her I could call him anytime.

Maybe it was wrong of me, and maybe it was just me running away again, but I decided, even after that, never to phone him. I had done what I felt was right for us at the time, but I didn't see any good in opening up old wounds. At the end of the day he had been the one that made the decision not to be involved, all those years ago.

So I gave the new information I had to the adoption agency and decided to let them take it from there.

*

A couple of weeks passed when I received another phone call from Mag. It was late one evening and I was racing around with Jessica in my arms trying to single-handedly prepare the dinner, as many mothers do.

"Hi, Mag, how are things going your end?"

"Not the least complicated I have dealt with to be honest." Her tone made me nervous.

"Would you be able to make yourself available if I was to come and meet with you tomorrow?"

"Of course" I replied, increasingly worried.

"Dan will be away with work tomorrow though and Jack has started back to school after the holidays, so it would only be myself at home."

"That actually works out perfectly, Aoife. We may have an issue and I would prefer, for the moment, to speak to you by yourself. I don't think it is something we should get involved in over the phone, but I have been in contact with Adam. He has responded to our letter." She then stopped herself from saying any more.

"We can discuss it all in the morning," she reassured me. "How would 11am suit?"

I agreed and hung up the phone. My heart was racing.

A potential problem – what could that be?

I couldn't even think straight and began to panic, with every possible scenario going through my mind. Dan came through the door soon after and I told him about the call I had just received, so we both sat down, forgetting about dinner, and just imagining every possible outcome. All we could come up with, however, was that maybe he was contesting the adoption. But how could he possibly do that without ever being a part of Jack's life? Would he really ruin this for us, for Jack, now? After all of these years it didn't make any sense and neither of us slept at all that night. It was so hard for Dan because he was already Jack's daddy in every other sense of the word and the fact that somebody else, who had never had any involvement, could stop it from becoming legal was heartbreaking.

I paced the kitchen all morning, waiting for Mag to come and fill me in on what was happening. And all the time those words, the ones he had crushed me with seven years ago, were ringing in my ears.

You will find someone to be a much better father to that child than I could ever be.

And I had! I had found the perfect father, so what were the issues now? This was all happening because of his decision seven years ago, not mine.

My train of thought was interrupted by the sound of the doorbell. Mag had finally arrived and I led her into the kitchen where we sat down to chat over a coffee.

"I am sure you are wondering why I needed to come and speak to you today," she began.

I couldn't hold my emotions in as I admitted to her, a little tearfully, that I was.

"A lot has come to light since I last saw you and there are some issues that we need to discuss before we can move forward with the adoption process."

This doesn't sound good, I thought, as I nervously sat on the edge of my seat, biting what was left of my nails.

And I couldn't believe what I was hearing.

"The form we had initially sent to Adam, outlining your plans for adoption, stated that it would take away any legal rights and responsibilities from him, over Jack. At the end of the form, where we requested Adam's signature, he has signed.

Right, that is a good thing, isn't it? I thought to myself. *Case closed, right?* Wrong.

"He has signed the letter alright, but unfortunately he has written a note under his signature stating that he didn't feel like he could ever really involve himself in Jack's life as he was never sure if he was really Jack's father."

I couldn't believe what I was hearing!

"Not sure if Jack was his?" I blurted out in shock. "In all of the years and all of the arguments we ended up having, this was never an issue, never a question!"

I couldn't believe it. Why was he being so underhanded now? There was never any question that he was Jacks father. He knew that, I knew he did. All he had to do for me, after everything I had to go through by myself, was sign this one form for me, for Jack, and then he could walk away forever if he wanted. But no, here he was again, standing in the way of me moving on with my life.

"I am trying to understand why he would have said that, but being honest this makes no sense," I said.

It was so frustrating and before long all the questions and the self blame crept in.

Did he really believe that? Is that really why he hadn't been involved? Apart from him initially asking if the baby was his, why had this never come up before, especially when it could have been sorted so easily?

I was heartbroken.

My whole childhood was shrouded in unanswered questions, in relation to my birth parents, and I had spent years trying to make sure my child wouldn't have to go through what I did.

If Adam really believed that he might not be the father then I felt sorry for him because he was living with that unknown and I knew exactly what that felt like. *But did he believe it? Or was he trying to make himself feel better about the fact that he had walked away?*

"You see, if there is any doubt, whatsoever, that Adam is Jack's birth father then we could not proceed with your application of adoption, because of the potential risk that another man may present himself, down the line, claiming to be the father. If that were the case we would have allowed an adoption to take place without his consent and that cannot happen."

"This is all very confusing, Adam is Jack's father. I don't know what else I can say. I understand your point of view, but I can't believe that one little note at the end of a form, from somebody who has never been there, could stop us from making Dan Jack's legal father. A note that has no truth."

I raised my hands up to my temples as I tried to get my head around the mess. This wasn't what I had been expecting from Mag's visit at all.

"What is the next step?" I eventually said. "This has become a 'my word against his' situation and I understand you can't just sweep it under the carpet."

"I realise this is hard, but try not to get downhearted, dear. These things are very rarely straightforward. Maybe to show the board that you are genuine, and that there is not a question in your mind, you should, through me, offer Adam a DNA test."

What?! I wasn't comfortable with having to go to these lengths after everything else we had gone through, when he walked away; but if that is what it took, then that is what I would do.

"Ok Mag, I think you should contact him again and offer him the test. If this is what we need to do, to proceed, then so be it. Maybe then we can all get on with our lives."

I couldn't wait for Mag to leave, I was trying so hard to hold it together and all I wanted to do was crawl up into a ball on the floor and phone Dan.

Less than 24 hours later my phone rang again. It was Mag. She had made the call to Adam and offered the DNA test, but to my surprise, and hers, after making the initial statement he refused. He backtracked on what he had said and told her that he never said that he wasn't, he just had a doubt, and that it wasn't necessary to do a test.

So why did he do it in the first place?!

This was something I didn't and, never will, understand. My compassion for him was wavering, once again, and now I felt angry. But I couldn't let that take over so, instead, I focused on the positives; knowing that I did the right thing and that Dan and I could now move forward in our adoption process. Bit of a roller coaster detour, but we had come through and were finally back on the right track. Adam's involvement was finished with and I could now close that chapter of my life and move on with my family.

I decided during that week that now was the time to tell Jack about Adam once and for all.

*

A few days later as Jack, Jessica and I were driving up to Dublin to see my parents we began to speak about our family. Jessica had fallen asleep and Jack was counting up all of his aunts and uncles on my side of the family, and then on Dan's.

"Do you remember the way mummy is adopted, love?" I ventured.

"Yep, Nanny Mary wasn't ready to be a mummy and Gran and Granddad wanted a baby, so you swapped."

I smiled to myself at his innocence.

"Something like that, lovie. Do you remember the way you and me met Daddy together and he feel in love with both of us?"

"Yep," Jack replied, chewing on a sticky bar.

"Well, when everyone is born we all have a mummy and a daddy."

"But Gran wasn't your mummy when you were born, Mary was, so was Granddad your daddy when you were first born?"

"No, lovie, somebody else was, but I didn't know who he was. I know his name is John."

"Did he not want to be your daddy mummy?"

"It was a little bit more complicated, lovie. What I am trying to say is you

148

are just like me, you had a different daddy too when you were born."

"A different daddy? What was his name?"

" His name is Adam."

"Did he not want to be my daddy?"

"It is not always that easy. I just don't think he was ready to be one, love."

"Wow Mummy, we have a really big family, are we nearly at gran's yet? Uncle Carl said he would be there to play football with me and I brought my new football gloves."

I could not believe it was that simple. Kids really are amazing – so trusting and accepting. *I wish adults could be more like that sometimes,* I thought as we pulled into mum and dad's driveway where Jack hopped out and rushed to greet them at the door.

Jack

I have always known that I was adopted by my dad. It has always felt normal. When I did have any questions I would ask my mummy or daddy and we would talk about it. It was never really a big deal. My daddy has always been there for me. I could not ask for a better dad and I love him very much. I do not remember a time when my dad was not around. I am just glad he is here with me and mummy and my sisters. After all, families come in all different shapes.

Thank God we had no other major upsets in the adoption process from that point onwards. It had come to the time, however, for the adoption board to check all parts of our application before making a decision in relation to the information supplied. It had been a long and tough wait, but eventually Mag phoned again saying she was now ready to come out to our house for the final visit. She wanted to meet Jack and fill us in on what part of the process they had reached.

Mag came out the next week and, thankfully, it was a much more informal visit than the previous one. She spoke to Jack, Dan and I about the next step and told us that all of our paperwork had come through OK. All of the checks had been completed and all we had to do now was wait for a letter to come, giving us a time and date to go in front of the adoption board. There a final decision would be made and an adoption order would be either granted or denied.

Because adoption law in Ireland had not been updated in years, when we began our process, it had been explained to us that we could not just apply for Dan to adopt Jack and become a legal guardian. I had to apply at the same time to adopt him too! Apparently if Dan had made the application without me, I would, technically, be giving up my rights to Jack and giving them to Dan, so we had to make a joint application. It meant that although, legally, I was, in every way, Jack's birth mother, I would also be his adoptive mother. Strange, I know, but it didn't matter how many odd hoops we had to jump through to make everything legal, we would have done them all – and would do them again.

It wasn't long before the letter arrived and we were given the date and time to go in front of the board. We knew all of our paperwork had come through OK, but still, that day, we were both a bag of nerves.

We were asked to bring Jack with us, which we were very happy to do, as he had been involved in the entire process up to that point, so this would be a very special day for all of us. My mum and dad took Jessica for us that morning and Dan, Jack and I had travelled into Dublin hoping to receive the news we had been waiting so long for. We had arranged to meet my parents, Jessie and Carl at a restaurant for lunch that afternoon in the hope that we would have something to celebrate.

Dan, Jack and I sat in the waiting room, with baited breath.

"I don't know how my parents had the strength to go through this twice," I said. "At least we have Jack here with us. I honestly don't know how they did it."

"I wonder what they are going to say," Dan mused, while playing with Jack on his knee.

I could tell he was as nervous as I was, maybe more. He couldn't sit still and we were both watching the clock as the time of our appointment came and went.

Trying to distract himself Dan turned to Jack, "Go grab one of those books on the coffee table and we will have a read."

I sat in silence just watching them, Jack hanging on Dan's every word, as he acted out all the funny voices in the book. This amazing man, the love of my life, had become a father, daddy and best friend to my son right in front of my eyes and I couldn't think of a more beautiful sight. I just hoped the board could see it too.

Still, I realised in that moment, it didn't matter what anyone had to say in the room across the hall. It didn't matter if we had a piece of paper to prove it or not, nobody was going to take their special relationship away from them. Jack had what he needed already, a real daddy, and one that loved him with every breath that he had in his body.

We really didn't know what to expect when we walked through the double doors and into the boardroom, all I knew was that I wasn't nervous any-more. Dan and I smiled at each other as we both, at the same time, reached out to take Jack's hand and took in the huge room with a big oak board table, and five people in suits, sitting on the other side of it.

"Hello there, and hello to you young man, please, take a seat," said an older man, sat in the middle, with a smile. "We have been reviewing your application to adopt Jack and I realise it hasn't been a straightforward process, it rarely is to be honest, but I hope you understand that our priority, through all of this, had to be the welfare of the child and what is best for them. We couldn't allow ourselves to be put in a situation where there was any doubt over the paternity and after we had the information it had to be reviewed, very carefully, to determine the right decision for Jack and everyone else involved."

Jack began to fidget in his seat, which drew the man's attention to him.

"Do you like my tie?"

He flipped his plain blue tie around to show Jack a picture of the Roadrunner on the other side.

"I love that cartoon," Jack replied with confidence.

I smiled as I recognised their attempt to make him feel comfortable, after all it was a situation that could have been very daunting for a little boy. The lady sitting directly in front of me, who was holding some papers in her hand, then said, "When all was said and done, and after we were fully satisfied that all of our questions had been answered, we came to our conclusion... and we are delighted to be here with an adoption order granting your application."

What?! Just like that? I couldn't believe it was over so quickly!

Almost immediately I let out a huge sigh of relief, before turning to Dan, who was holding our son's hand tighter than ever, with tears in his eyes.

He knew he was already Jack's daddy, but now he was his legal guardian too. He was his first-born child and I knew right then that this was to be the most special day of his life.

"Thank you so much," Dan and I said in unison.

"All that is left to say is congratulations!" The lady said as every member of the board grinned at us broadly.

With that, Dan lifted his son up in his arms and we walked out of the office. It was an amazing feeling, one none of us will ever forget, and we couldn't wait to go get Jessie, meet my folks and tell them the news. I really felt that I was, for the first time, able to fully close off that chapter of my life.

Now it was time to write a new one.

Dan

From the very first day I laid eyes on Aoife, I was smitten. Love at first sight and all that! What I didn't expect was to fall in love with the full package. I mean that Aoife did not just come alone. She also had a beautiful son. Our first dates were very different to your average first dates. We spent a lot of time in Dublin Zoo with Jack and he and I would have fun making all the animal noises every time we passed them.

When I met Jack for the first time I was very nervous. It was like a job interview! I thought to myself that if this little child didn't like me, screamed when I went near him or hit me if I tried to lift him, then Aoife would run for sure. So to keep our relationship on track, I had to impress this little man. Well I pulled out all the stops! Making an idiot of myself to make him laugh, singing the Barney song and running around like a mad man. By the end of the day Jack and I were getting along great and I didn't have to try anymore. We just clicked.

So, you see, to become Aoife's boyfriend (and then husband), I had to get the thumbs up from Aoife and Jack and I was delighted that I passed the test… eventually!

As time moved on, Jack and I were just like every other father and son. I was dad and I always called Jack my son. Well he is my son. After all, what is the definition of a dad? Is it the person who gets a woman pregnant? Is it the man whose name is on the birth certificate? I don't think so. A dad is the man who is there for every birthday. The man who puts his son to bed at night. The man who looks out for him every day, attends every school play, watches him play his football matches, brings him to his friend's birthday parties (and trust me, there are a lot of these) and most importantly, the man who loves him no matter what.

Anyone can be a father, but I'm more happy to be his dad. In my heart Jack has always been my son, but in the eyes of the state he wasn't. I always spoke with Aoife about adopting Jack and it was something we agreed to do once we were married. Aoife would tell me about how her parents adopted her, so I knew it was not going to be easy, but I had no idea just how hard it really was going to be. All the questions! It felt like I was captured behind enemy lines and was being interrogated. But at the end of the day, this is what had to be done and I was going to do whatever was needed. Our hard work and patience paid off and eventually the day came to meet the adoption board. To be honest, I would consider myself to be a brave person. I was a trained soldier, spent months overseas on UN missions, running around the jungle on covert ops, I was also a trained fire-fighter and tackled a blaze or two in my time, but this was the most frightening experience of my life. What if they said NO? How would we move forward from this? So many times I thought, Dear God I'm going to pass out … and I nearly did! I remember walking up into the waiting area, hyperventilating and looking as grey as the cement walls. "Come on Danny, get a grip" I kept saying to myself. "If they say no, Jack is still your son." But I still wanted, so badly, for it to be a yes. I wanted Jack to know when he is older that I went through this for him. For us.

"Jack Curran," the lady called.

"Yes, that's us," I said, while getting to my feet. My legs like jelly.

We were directed into this room with the biggest table in the world and all the "business-looking" people seated behind. What happened next is very much a blur. I thought I was going to lose it, so I had to busy myself playing with Jack. The only part of that meeting that I remember is hearing that they had decided to grant our adoption order and I just looked at Jack and in my head said, "That's it Jack. Now I truly am your dad, even in the eyes of the state."

When all is said and done, it is a great thing to meet a beautiful woman with an amazing child. If they both don't think that you are up for the job, you're sacked! Aoife got to find out in advance what I was going to be like as a husband and a dad. Thank God they both said YES.

Chapter 21 – Here we go again!

LIFE got back to normal fairly quickly after the adoption went through. It was a relief not to have to wait for the phone to ring. At that time I thought a lot about my parents, when they were going through the adoption process, and as hard as it was for us, I reminded myself that we still had Jack with us every step of the way. When we were waiting for the postman, we were playing with him and we were still putting him to bed every night. We were still mummy and daddy – but when my folks were going through the process, they hadn't yet got a child to love, to put to bed or play with. They were waiting for someone to tell them that they were good enough to be parents, and it must have taken some strength to get through those interviews, not knowing if a child would ever call them mummy and daddy – not knowing if they would ever have a little hand to hold tight. It was then that I truly realised how strong they really were.

While we had been going through the adoption process ourselves and talk of fathers, birth fathers and adoptive fathers, was rife, thoughts of my own birth father kept creeping into my mind. More and more I had been thinking about it, especially as our family grew, and no matter what way I looked at it, I just couldn't accept that it was meant to be that John had never known about me. That he still didn't know about me, and that it wasn't his choice. I wanted him to at least be given the chance to feature in my life, so I decided to do something about it.

I went back to my original notes from the adoption agency and between those and what Mary had told me since, I pieced together all of the information I had about him, in an effort to get a clue about where to start my search.

I decided very early on, that I wasn't going to use the adoption agency this time, that if I could find him myself I would try; and if I couldn't, then it wasn't meant to be. I remembered all the fuss they made surrounding meeting Mary, and I just didn't want to go there again. I wanted to do things my way and to make it more real from the start. So I sat Dan down, over a bottle of wine one night, when the kids had gone to bed, and told him I felt ready to try and find my birth father. Typically he was right on board and immediately got out a piece of paper and asked me to tell him everything I knew about John, before exclaiming, "I will find him for you!"

So we collated the information we had. I knew that John was in and around the same age as Mary when I was born. I knew he had a love of hurling and music, that he had brown hair and was from the west of Ireland. Mary thought that she had heard, in the years after, that he had got married. This was something, I have to admit, I was worried about. The last thing I wanted to do was upset anyone's life or marriage by turning up saying, "Hi, I'm the daughter you never knew about."

It had the potential to cause a lot of upset.

So I knew I had to tread as carefully as possible and try to find out as much as I could before I revealed to anybody who I was. I just didn't want to cause any trouble and I didn't think this man owed me anything, especially having not even known of my existence for twenty six years. So Dan and I came up with a plan, to phone the family business and say we were looking to contact John in order to organise a reunion between a group of friends.

Dan found the number fairly easily and with the phone in his hand told me not to worry that he would ring and find out what he could. It was John's brother who answered the phone. This man would have been my uncle if things had been different; and it was difficult to get that straight in my head. It was like a sliding doors moment, when you come face to face with a life that could have been, if different decisions had been made in the past.

I listened as Dan said that he was looking to contact John for a reunion and the conversation flowed for a few minutes. The resulting information did help us, but unfortunately not enough to get us closer to contacting him. John and his brother had lost touch over the years and he was no longer living in the country. He was married to a woman from the area and had three kids, the eldest of which was very close to my age, only two years between us, but, the man explained, they hadn't very much contact with him either. He wasn't sure if they would have an up-to-date address for John either. It wasn't what I had been hoping to hear, but at least we found out that I had more half brothers and sisters, which was both amazing and difficult at the same time.

John's brother gave Dan an old phone number he had for him and told us he was not sure if that was still current, but it was all he had, before wishing us luck on our search. Good news and bad news all at the same time. I had more family out there, but it was looking like John would be hard to find.

We didn't do anything more for the next couple of weeks, as not long after Jessica was born, I decided that I wanted to become an Emergency Medical Technician so all the study was keeping me busy. I had always wanted to work on an ambulance and I was really enjoying what I was doing. Admittedly I was in two minds about my search at that point anyway. I think I was afraid of what I might find. Was I luring myself into a lion's den? We got the impression that John's children were still in Ireland and he didn't see much of them but had we taken up that information right? Or were we reading too much into things? It was possible that his brother just didn't want to give too much information out to a stranger on the phone. Either way I was confused, but I came to the decision in the end that all of those questions took up more space in my head than the answers ever would, so we set about continuing our search.

One afternoon Dan rang me from work. I was waiting to pick Jack up from school and trying to keep Jessie entertained in the car when he said bluntly, "Facebook Aoife, if he had children close to your age, they are probably on Facebook. You know his surname and it is slightly unusual, so why don't you put a search into Facebook?" I couldn't believe I hadn't thought of this myself.

"Could finding lost family really be as simple as looking up a Facebook account?"

"All you can do is try, babe."

"I'll do it as soon as I get home," I said, a little excited. "I will let you know if I come up with anything."

As soon as I got home I took out the laptop and typed in the surname and only one page of people came up. Second from the top a girl grabbed my attention.

This must be somebody related to him. Same name, living in exactly the right town in the right part of the county. *Would it really be that easy?* I thought to myself. I knew it wasn't John, but it was as close as it got right then if she was the right person. I waited for Dan to come home and we sat down together to figure out what we would do with this new piece of the puzzle. We finally decided I would send her a private message and try to confirm who she was, without revealing who I was. I didn't want to hurt anyone or disrupt anyone's life, so it took me all night to compile the message despite it being simple and short.

> Hi,
> By any chance would your dad or uncle maybe be called John?
> I think we may have been family friends when I was a child
> and I have just come across you on Facebook and was wondering if I had the right person.

Every day in work, out on the ambulance, whenever we had Wi-Fi, I would take out my laptop and check to see if I had a response to my message. Two, three, then four days passed and no response, until one evening, after we'd

dropped a patient off at a Dublin hospital, I took out my laptop expecting more of the same, when a message flashed up at the top of my page. The Wi-Fi was slow, so it felt like it took forever for the message to open. It was her! I was almost afraid to open it. *What would she think with a stranger writing her this message? Would she think I was some lunatic off the Internet?*
There was only one way to find out.

She was very friendly in her message back and told me that, yes, John was her dad. I had found my half sister and all it took in the end was a quick search on Facebook! She didn't seem to think it was strange that I had contacted her; she just said she felt really bad that she didn't remember who I was, but that my face seemed familiar to her. She told me that her dad had moved away some years ago and he and her mother weren't together anymore, but she was trying to place where we had met. She didn't have much contact with her dad these days…

Right, it was time for the truth!

Now that I knew I wasn't going to be causing trouble in a marriage I felt it wasn't right not to tell her the truth and I had nothing to lose by telling her. I was relieved that I could tell her exactly who I was too.

Right, I guess I should start at the beginning. But before I do I just want to say that I hope I don't put you in an awkward position. Here it goes. My name is Aoife. I am married and I have two kids. Twenty-seven years ago, I was put up for adoption and I grew up in Dublin. When I turned twenty I got in touch with my birth mother, whose name is Mary. She and my birth father were in a relationship and were around the same age. She never told my birth father she was pregnant with me and still, to this day, he does not know about me. She told me my birth father was your dad John. I am sure after that last sentence you haven't a clue what to think. I am sorry for landing this all on you now. I really don't want to upset anybody. I guess it is just hard having a blank family history and not knowing where you came from. For my kids, right now, family history stops with me. I really hope that I have not upset you. I have battled with myself trying to decide whether or not to send this and I would totally understand if you do not want to reply.

Thanks so much.

Aoife.

It didn't take days for a response this time – she answered pretty much straight away.

Hi Aoife,

I couldn't believe it, as I read every word of your message. I hope your life is good. Things haven't always been easy with our family and my dad. I am so glad I know about you now, writing to me mustn't have been easy. I am not sure how much I can help as Dad and I haven't really spoken much over the past few years. I think we have both moved on with our lives. He is alive and well and living in Europe with a new family. You do have more half brothers and sisters between here and Europe. Between us here and his family there, there are six of us.

I really hope you were adopted into a nice family and your life has worked out well. I am still in shock here!

If there is anything else I can do to help let me know.

After we got to know each other's circumstances a little bit, I sent her one last message back, thanking her for being so open to me and understanding. I left her my phone number if she ever wanted to get in touch and I told her that, thanks to her, I now knew a lot more about the pieces of the puzzle surrounding my past and that I felt closure for the first time. I didn't know it would be, but when it came down to it, talking to her was enough for me. I didn't feel the need to continue my search for John. She had filled me in with as much as I needed to know and I told her that I would no longer be trying to find him. She had helped me more than I thought possible, by simply sending a few messages, but it was time for me to let sleeping dogs lie and move on with my life. We wished one another well, and that was that. I had no clue if we would stay in touch, but I was so grateful to her for giving me the closure I couldn't get myself for the last twenty-seven years.

For the first time in my adoption journey I felt OK about not having all the answers and was able to move on with my life, being a wife, a mummy and a daughter with a full-time job in the ambulance service.

I was content.

Chapter 22 – "I think I'm your dad!"

ONE morning, about three weeks later, I was instructing a cardiac first response class in one of the private ambulance training centres that just happened to be in the west, close to where my birth father was from. It was a normal busy day and I was demonstrating how to perform CPR, to the students on a mannequin, when my phone rang. It was on silent in my pocket so I didn't answer the call but just one minute later it rang again… and then a third time. I took it out and didn't recognise the number, an international one, but I wondered if it might be important, as whoever it was, seemed fairly eager to contact me. Still, they didn't leave a voicemail.

Then it rang again.

"Hello?"

"Hi, is this Aoife?"

"Yep, that's me. How can I help?"

"I think I'm your dad!"

The room started to spin. Could I really just have answered the phone to my birth father? As strange as it sounds he had totally caught me off guard and I was confused, so the only thing I could think of to say was, "Are you sure you have the right number?"

"I have been away from Ireland for a long time and over the years have had contact with my family on and off. I haven't spoken to them in around a year but my daughter phoned me this morning and told me about you. I am in shock to be honest. I haven't seen Mary in years.

I didn't even know she had a child! My daughter told me that hearing from you and knowing what she now knows that she couldn't keep it to herself so she thought the right thing to do was to tell me."

I hadn't even considered that a possibility, as his daughter had told me they no longer spoke and I had told her that I wouldn't take my search any further. *Could this really be happening?* He sounded so welcoming on the phone and told me he was delighted to hear about me. This was too much and on the day I happened to be in the town where he was from!

Coincidence or fate?

There was that question again. It was hard for me to take in let alone believe. I was in shock but barely managed to say, "I am in the middle of teaching a class so I can't really speak at the minute, but I can phone you back on this number this evening if that is ok?"

Not able to talk? I couldn't believe I said that, but I had to get off the phone. This was too huge. I needed some time to comprehend what had just happened. I got off the phone as soon as I could and phoned Dan. He couldn't believe what had just happened, and I was getting panicky.

I don't know how I got through the rest of the day in the class, but I was also glad to have a distraction from it all. Before I knew it I was driving home, with thoughts of him weighing heavily on my mind. I talked on the phone to Dan for nearly an hour, going over things and trying to work out what I was going to say; because even though I had experienced adoption from every angle, this had to be the strangest, most difficult experience of my story so far.

I finally found the courage to dial the number and he answered after just one ring. He genuinely sounded very pleased to hear from me as he told me how happy he was that I had got in touch.

Throughout the length of the call I explained to him all about Mary and how it was that I came to learn about him, and he filled me in on parts of his life. More brothers and sisters! As well as having three children in Ireland, he now also had three kids in Europe, where he now lived. As it turned out John was also adopted, so he was very interested in my story because he had attempted to trace his own birth parents, but had not had any success in doing so.

It was one of the most surreal experiences of my life. Between Mary and John, I now had eight half brothers and sisters! My daughter was the same age as his youngest child too! I didn't know how to feel, but I was grateful at his kind response in finding out about me and decided I would just let myself go with it. I had nothing to lose.

I was over the moon at how well that first contact had gone, but in a strange way I was also glad that he was in Europe and not Ireland, as I had grown up a lot since meeting Mary and becoming a parent myself, and I knew it would not be good for any of us to rush into a meeting. We all needed time to let what had happened sink in and just get to know each other, a little bit first, over the phone.

I sat down with Dan that night, over a cup of tea at the kitchen table, and filled him in on the day's events. He couldn't believe that after everything, it had been as simple as Facebook leading me to him. Suddenly, our conversation was interrupted by my phone ringing again – it was John. God he was keen, it hadn't been an hour since we had hung up from our first conversation.

I thought it was a bit strange, but he was just so eager to find out more about me that he wanted me to add him as a friend on Facebook so he could see some pictures. I didn't stay on the phone long that time, but I did what he had asked and said goodbye. It was only after the second call that Mary popped into my head and I suddenly realised that I hadn't filled her in on what had been happening. At the end of the day, it wasn't just my past that I was dragging up, it was hers too and John was part of a very hard time in Mary's life. I phoned her straight away and I could hear the disbelief in her voice. She was, however, so supportive and happy that I had got the best re-action I could hope for from him and she said she would like to write him a message and try to explain how all of this had come about. She hoped that might help him understand how and why things unfolded the way they did all those years ago. I gave Mary a link to his Facebook account as she con-sidered her own next step.

To say the next few days were a whirlwind would be an understatement. Between calls from Mary telling me John had answered a message from her and shown the same understanding; to several calls from John to me, it was all go!

One Wednesday, I was up early for my shift on the ambulance, which had started at 6am, when my phone rang. *Who could possibly be phoning me at six in the morning?* I quickly took my phone from my jacket pocket thinking something must be wrong, when I saw that it was John's number. I answered straight away and noticed he seemed very hyper as he told me he had a sur-prise for me. He was at the airport and was coming home to meet me.

I couldn't believe what I was hearing and I wasn't sure it was a good idea to rush things like this, but he was at the airport, what could I say? He asked me to come and meet him in Dublin at lunchtime, but I was just starting a ten-hour shift, which saved me from having to agree. I needed some time to pre-pare for this, but it looked like time was not on my side. After so many years of waiting, so many years of not knowing, I might be expected to jump at the opportunity, but rushing things like this, for some reason, left me feeling uneasy. I wanted to plan things properly. I wanted to do things the right way.

What should I say?

I tried not to show him my concern over the phone, as I knew the effort he had already gone to, and I couldn't help but think I had brought this on myself, but as soon as I got a break on the ambulance I phoned Mary. I could always be honest with her and I knew she would understand why I was wor-ried. She reassured me that when she had known him, that he was a lovely guy, the life and soul of the party, but she understood my concerns. So, she asked me if it would help if she went and met him by herself that night so I could take some time to get my head around it. She would then come with me to meet him again, the next day. I was so grateful for Mary's support, which allowed me exactly what I needed. Time. I also knew that Mary and

John would have their own issues to discuss and it would be better to get all of that out in the open before I met him. Mary was my lifesaver that day. She put herself in the line of fire to save me from feeling uncomfortable.

The next day came all too quickly. Mary and John's first meeting after twenty-seven years had gone unexpectedly well and it was now my turn to meet my birth father for the first time.

Mary had warned me that John was fond of a drink, but she had made him promise her that when she brought me to meet him, that it would be during the day and he wouldn't have had a drink so we could talk properly. He was happy to agree and it was decided that we would meet in the lounge of a hotel at 4pm. Myself and Dan picked Mary up at 3.30pm and as we were running about twenty minutes late I sent John a text to inform him, saying we would be in touch as soon as we reached town. On the way in Mary filled us in on how her night had gone, in an attempt to explain to me what I should expect from him, and I was getting more and more nervous. I had to talk myself out of turning the car around at one point. *What was wrong with me?* I had wanted this for so long, but had never had these concerns when I met Mary. I told myself it was just nerves and as I pulled into the Brown Thomas car park Mary called him. He told her that he had got so nervous waiting for us that he was no longer in the lounge of the hotel and had popped around the corner to the pub, "to have a drink to calm his nerves." He then asked if we would meet him there.

A drink? This now had the potential to go very wrong. I was beginning to miss the limitations that the adoption agency had put on us. *Did he not understand how important this first meeting was?* After everything I had imagined over the years, meeting my birth father in a pub for the first time definitely was not what I had envisaged. Mary was fuming with him, but what could we do now, so we changed direction and headed for the bar.

As we reached the door Dan took one look at my struggling face and grabbed my hand.

"Its OK, babe. We will go in and give him the benefit of the doubt, and if you are in any way uncomfortable we will leave, but you have come too far not to try. I'm here all the way."

That was enough for me and we walked through the pub and up the stairs towards the smoking area. I would be lying if I said it felt right. It didn't, it felt very wrong. My heart was beating so fast, but I forced myself to put one foot in front of the other. The one thing I hadn't been expecting was that John might bring a friend with him for support yet there they were, sat there telling everyone else in the smoking area that he was about to meet his daughter for the first time.

When I finally built up the courage to open that door he walked toward me and I got a standing ovation from the crowd. Everybody was staring and clapping, but I just felt like running.

The first moment we ever laid eyes on each other should have been a special one, and done in private. *How did it happen that I was now sharing the first time I ever met my birth farther with a pub full of strangers?* Before we had even sat down he handed me a box with a necklace inside. It was beautiful and a lovely thought, but I couldn't even take it in those surroundings. We found a seat in the corner, but there was no getting away from all the eyes staring at us. John sat beside me and held my hand, and I found myself wishing for the option of that table between us, that the adoption agency had offered when I met Mary. I had thought it so unnecessary then, but I would have given anything for the social worker, Ann, to be there forcing him to take things slowly and give me my space (which is ironic because all I wanted when I met Mary, under those circumstances, was to get away from that). But John didn't understand and I didn't know how to make him understand. I needed that table, I needed that social worker popping her head around the door and I needed my space.

I found myself unable to speak to him. I didn't know what to say. Mary recognised this in me straight away and filled in all of the potentially awkward silences. Both she and Dan did the best they could to help ease the tension while John chatted away the whole time. I just couldn't get myself to relax.

I was still sitting there, silent but surrounded by everyone else's conversation, when John's friend came over to our table and sat down beside me, kissing my hand. To say he had a few drinks on him would have been an understatement and I didn't pass too much notice of him until, without saying a word, he put his head down on the table. I didn't know what to think so I pushed my chair away from him and looked at Dan and Mary pleadingly. Before anyone had time to react though, this guy that my birth father thought would be a suitable person to accompany him while meeting me for the first time, proceeded to get sick all over my shoes.

How could this be happening?

It was a total disaster and Mary had seen enough. Taking John aside she told him we were leaving and that if he wanted to ever have any type of relationship with me, he should come with us for some food, and sober up. He apologised for his friend and left the pub with us, but to be honest, I didn't even know if I wanted him there anymore.

Once we were away from the pub and his drunken friend, however, I began to relax a little bit and we did end up having a good chat in the Chinese restaurant. It wouldn't have happened without Mary and Dan, and despite having the most disastrous start imaginable, as the evening went on, I began to see that he didn't mean any harm. He just found it difficult to identify the boundaries, because he never knew about his "long lost daughter," and I could tell he wanted a close relationship with me almost instantly. I found this hard to face. It had come so naturally to Mary and I when we met, but I wasn't getting the seem feeling with John.

And besides, I had a dad, the most amazing dad in the world, and one was all I needed. So as much as I wanted to find John and meet him to fill in the blanks, it was apparent that a father/daughter relationship was not on the cards for me.

We finished our meal and I told John it was time for us to go as my parents had been looking after the kids for us, for the entire afternoon and it was getting late. John had said early in the evening that he would be in Ireland for a couple of days and wanted to meet me again before he flew out. I wasn't comfortable meeting him on my own though, and Dan and Mary were both working; so I told him we both had a lot to take in and asked if it was OK if we waited until the next time he flew home to meet up again.

As the words came out of my mouth I saw the tears build up in his eyes – he knew it was time to say goodbye. I felt so bad, but I had to be true to myself and I was just too overwhelmed.

When he gave me a hug he didn't let go and, again, I longed for Ann to pop her head around the door and insist on some space, but no Ann this time, just a homeless guy who had caught John's eye over my shoulder and asked him if he had any spare change. John let go of me then to root through his pocket for a fiver, which he handed over to the man, before putting his arm him and saying, "Come on and I will buy you a pint, I could do with one too."

Then he was gone, down Grafton Street, arm in arm with a man he'd never met.

I had an eventful few weeks after that with a lot of messages and phone calls from John. His daughters in Europe also made contact with me and welcomed me to the family; and in the middle of all the madness, out of the blue, my half sister in Galway phoned and I was delighted to finally get to talk to her also. It was amazing. There were no awkward silences and I was able to chat with both my half sisters like they were friends. They also explained a little bit about the ups and downs of their relationship with John over the years, which helped me to make sense of some of my feelings. It wasn't long before we decided that we all wanted to meet up, so Dan and I drove down one afternoon, close to where they are from, and met them in a hotel. I wasn't as nervous this time, as I had been for other meetings. We had got to know each other the right way, over the phone and via messages first, so it felt more normal and relaxed.

We had a great afternoon, filling each other in on our lives and I felt better, too, hearing their stories of reuniting with John. It turned out that there was a period of around ten years when they hadn't seen him either, so they had only recently had a reunion of their own with him. I told them about how my first meeting had gone with him and we all had a good laugh over a coffee. By the end of the day we had decided that the next time John flew into the country, we would all go and meet him together, so we could support and take the pressure off each other. I was so much happier with this and on the drive home I couldn't help but think of all the new people that had come into my life over the past few years. Mary, Mick and their two kids had become such important people to me, and now I knew John and had met two of his daughters. There are so many adopted people out there who never get any of the answers to those important questions and I knew then, that whatever way it was to turn out with John, I was very lucky.

Only a few weeks had passed when I got another call from John telling me he was coming to Ireland again in two weeks' time and asking if I might be free to meet him, joking that he was trying to give me notice this time around. So I spoke to his daughters on the phone and we arranged a day that we were all free to go and meet him together. I wanted, however, to meet with them beforehand, as I had some news, so mum and dad came down to look after the kids and Dan and I headed back towards the west.

As soon as we arrived I told my half sisters that our next baby was on the way and I was so thrilled by how supportive and delighted they were to hear it. We then phoned John and, surprise surprise, he was waiting for us in a pub. It was decided that we wouldn't spend any time in the pub when we arrived to meet John and that we would tell him we were leaving straight away to go and have some lunch, in order to avoid a repeat performance of the last time. When we got there he was happy to leave with us, but had another friend in tow. This one was sober, thankfully, and so was John so we headed off down the road to a little restaurant where we got something to eat. During the meal Dan and I told John our news. He was so happy for us and things were beginning to look up, with me feeling more and more like I could open up to him and speak normally. That day was so much more comfortable than the first and the girls were amazing, helping everyone to relax. It suited me that John no longer lived in Ireland as it forced space and time between us, without me having to ask for it and upset him. I had my life, family and pregnancy to keep me busy and I was happy in the thought that the next few weeks would be full of excitement.

I was approaching my first scan, which happened to be on my birthday, and I couldn't wait.

Chapter 23 – Never forgotten

I WAS so excited the morning of my scan. Dan took the day off work and we drove up to Dublin together. We hadn't told the kids about the baby, as we weren't yet in the safe zone, so we dropped them off with my mum and headed to the hospital. We were only waiting a couple of minutes when we were called in to the dark room and I excitedly hopped up on the bed as the sonographer made polite conversation with us, asking how long we had known we were expecting and if we had any other children. She then squirted the gel on my stomach and proceeded to move the monitor around.

I could see fairly quickly, when the picture popped up on the screen, that something wasn't right, and as soon as she asked if I had, in fact, had a positive pregnancy test and if I was certain that my dates were right, it was pretty clear.

"There is no heartbeat," she said. "I'm so sorry, but it looks like you have lost your baby."

There are no words to convey how devastated we were. Heartbroken and utterly lost, don't even come near.

Our world came crashing down around us and we needed to get out of there. I couldn't breathe and I couldn't stop the tears from streaming down my face. *How could this happen to me? Why me? Why now?* I will never forget the look of pity on the sonographer's face. It was something I'm sure, in her job, she was used to having to tell people, but she still showed me as much compassion as if it were the first time she ever had to say those words.

And for that, in the depths of my grief, I was so thankful.

Before we could leave, which we were desperate to do, she told us that there were procedures we had to follow in order to confirm the miscarriage. I had to go and have a blood test and then a repeat test within forty eight hours, in order to identify that my hormone levels were lowering, which would confirm the loss of our child. Like a zombie I let them take my blood and arranged a follow up appointment. Dan held my hand tight and we both walked to the car in silence. Both of our sets of parents had been waiting eagerly by the phone for news of how the scan had gone, and we knew we had to get it over with, so Dan and I each phoned our own parents as we sat in the car park. Afterwards we both remained in the car holding each other, and crying over our lost baby.

Dan took the rest of the week off work to be with me and come to my next blood test. We were just going through the motions, but supporting each other as much as we could and trying to keep things as normal as possible for the kids. I just wanted to get that test over with and get through whatever the next step was to be. After the test was over we left the hospital as soon as we could, deciding to go for a coffee in a nearby café, before travelling home. We sat there, on a beautiful spring day, trying to hold it together while listening to all the other normal conversations going on around us, about work, weddings and nights out. Our conversation wasn't normal though, and it wasn't happy, so we were leaning into each other across the table and speaking very low, trying to keep from getting upset again and avoid anyone hearing us.

"I just want this over, Dan, I can't cope with all of this waiting, it seems so cruel. How could I have lost our baby? I still feel pregnant, I am a mother you would think I would know if my baby wasn't alive?"

Holding back the tears Dan forced a sympathetic smile.

"Things don't always work out that way, my love. I wish the world was that simple, but sometimes, bad things happen to good people and there is nothing we can do about that. We will get through whatever life throws at us though, together. I promise"

Just then my phone rang. It was the hospital. We had been expecting them to call when the results came through and I had to find the strength to hold it together and answer the call. It wasn't the nurse I was expecting, but a man's voice that came over the phone.

"Is this Aoife?"

"That's right," I replied

"I am one of the consultants from the hospital. We were surprised to find that your recent blood tests showed your hormone levels have significantly increased, which is why I am phoning you."

"I am confused; the nurse had explained to me that they were only doing the blood tests to confirm my levels had decreased, which would confirm the miscarriage. They have increased? What does that mean?"

His next words would lift me from my pit of despair and give me hope where, just moments before, I believed there to be none.

"Quite simply it means that there is a possibility that you may still be pregnant. Your levels are right on track for your gestation, so it is possible that your baby just implanted later then we had thought. I would like you to come in and see me for a repeat scan, and for your own peace of mind we should do this sooner rather than later. Would you be free to make your way to see me now?"

I couldn't believe what I was hearing. *Could I still have my baby?* Dan and I raced from the coffee shop to the hospital, where we met the consultant.

We didn't get any major confirmation from the second scan but at least we had hope. It turned out that my hormone levels were a great indication that I still had my baby, and the best thing to do would be to wait three weeks and return for a repeat scan.

Three weeks? How would I get through three weeks? But I knew I could, when I had hope. I would keep reminding myself, *we might still have our baby.*

My only way of coping during those three weeks was to block everything else out and try to focus on my kids, my family and how I was feeling – so John's constant phone calls became unbearable. He kept saying that he shouldn't be made to feel that it was wrong to want to speak to me every day, that I was "his blood." He wanted to be involved, but I felt like he was forcing things. I had only met him twice and I didn't feel ready to open up about how I was feeling to anyone other than my mum and dad. I knew his intentions were good, but I couldn't cope, so I asked him for time and space – something he didn't take too well.

I didn't know if I was coming or going during that time. It was the most difficult experience of my life to date, and I had no room for anything else, so when John refused to listen to my requests for space, I began to avoid some of his calls. Maybe it wasn't the right thing to do, but it was my way of coping at the time.

Eventually our three-week wait was over and the night before the scan arrived. We had been in limbo, thinking our baby was gone then believing that there might be a chance our baby was still there. We hadn't known how to act or feel – we just kept praying that everything would work out OK; but when I experienced the most awful pain, low down in my stomach, that night, we finally knew that it wasn't.

It was like nothing I had ever felt before and I just knew that was it. I knew I had lost my baby.

We had come so far, with so many ups and downs. We had even come through the three weeks, but now, the day before my scan, I had lost my baby. It seemed so cruel, so unfair and our hopes, along with our little person, died that day.

I can't think of an appropriate word to describe the sense of loss and grief we felt buried under. Grief can do strange things to people, but thank God with Dan and I, if anything, it brought us closer together. I had to go into hospital to have a small procedure and he was with me every step of the way. In the days, weeks and months that followed we were there for each other and slowly I was able to accept I may not have my baby to hold in my arms, but I will always have my baby to hold in my heart.

I didn't know how I was going to face people again as any broaching of the subject with my family just brought tears so Dan and I decided between us, that apart from our parents, we would send everyone else a message telling them what had happened. We knew they would understand.

We needed space and time to come to terms with our loss and I told them I would speak about it when I felt stronger. We received so many messages of support from everyone, but sadly John was the only person who didn't react well to us. We hadn't known but he had flown into Ireland without telling us and had come to Kildare wanting to see me. He told me that he expected more than a message and that I owed that to him. I was so angry. Maybe it was my grief presenting itself in a different way, but I saw red! He was putting pressure on me now, so I picked up the phone and we ended up having a big argument. He just couldn't understand why I needed space, so in no uncertain terms I ended up telling him that if he wanted to be a part of my life he would back off and give me the time I needed, with my family, to come to terms with our loss. If he couldn't understand that, then maybe he should not be a part of my life.

I hung up the phone, hoping I had got through to him and spent the next few weeks getting the support I needed form Dan and the kids.

About a month had passed when I found myself realising that I must have got through to John because he hadn't been phoning me every day and eventually I began to feel like I was ready to speak to him again. It was all going well for about a week when one night I was lying awake in bed at about 2am. Jessie had come into us saying she couldn't sleep so I had just settled her back to bed and was drifting off myself when my phone rang. It was John. I thought something must be wrong if he was calling me that time of the morning so I answered, but as soon as I did I realised that he was drunk.

How could this man I still barely knew not realise that this was not normal? I knew he didn't mean any harm, but was he ever going to listen to me or respect my feelings?

After a short conversation I realised there was no point in trying to reason with him, so I told him it was too late to speak and I would ring him the next day. I waited until lunchtime and when I got through I set some boundaries. Straight away I made my feelings clear, saying that it was not OK to ring me from the pub at 2am because I worked full-time and was a busy mother. If he called me once and left a message, I would get back to him as soon as I could and there was no need to repeatedly call me the same day. I knew he was insecure, but this wasn't the right way to go about helping our new relationship.

He listened to me and said that he sometimes felt I didn't want to speak to him so I tried to explain that from my experiences getting to know Mary, you had to take the process slowly or it would never work.

Had I finally got through to him?

I was so happy that I had the courage to speak up, believing that he had finally listened to me, but that was the only weekend that ended up passing uneventfully. The very next weekend, at 3am, my phone rang again. It was John.

How could we keep going around in circles?

At that stage I had gone through a phase of saying nothing, a phase of being angry with him, and even one of telling him, in no uncertain terms, to back off! But nothing was getting through to him.

Eventually I decided that if he ever phoned me after midnight again I would not answer or call him back. I would only answer when he phoned me at a decent hour.

I was expecting a call from him the next day, which to my surprise never came and I went on to get through a whole week without a call from him. So I left things as they were and wondered again what the weekend would bring. And what it brought was a 2.30am call.

This time, though, he left me an angry voice message reprimanding me for not answering him. I didn't sleep, at all, for the rest of the night, I was too angry.

No matter what I did, or what I said I could not get through to him and there was nothing left to do. I had tried every way I knew to get him to take things slow and listen to me, but it was a lost cause.

What was left, but to give up?

I was still battling with myself over how I was going to handle the situation when I realised that it had been a month without any contact from him. I hadn't phoned him and he hadn't phoned me. Maybe this was what was right, I reasoned. Maybe ours was a path I wasn't supposed to take. Maybe neither of us was able to stay in touch without the drama, so maybe we shouldn't *be* in touch. I had tried to have a relationship with John, but sometimes you have to just admit defeat and accept that some things aren't meant to be. I was happy with the conclusion, especially knowing that I had done everything I could and, finally, I felt closure.

It was as though I had come full circle, from the tiny baby left in the foster home to the grown woman, who didn't have all the answers, but had all the ones she needed.

Chapter 24 – Complete

AS life has a habit of doing, it moved on, and so did I.

Just over a year had passed and Dan and I found ourselves back down the same road that had caused us so much joy, but also so much sadness, in the past. We were expecting again and were so nervous when we found ourselves waiting outside the room for our first scan. This time it was the middle of summer and the sun was shining through the window when we walked through, hand in hand, to a very bright spacious room where we saw the beautiful beating heart of our third child, for the first time.

Grace Louise was born on the 22nd of February, 2012 at 5.30pm, weighing in at 7 pound, 8 ounces. She was perfect, but moments after she arrived I was filled with fear when I noticed that she wasn't crying – she wasn't even breathing. The nurses quickly snatched her from me and began forcing air into my tiny baby's body and finally, after what felt like an eternity I heard the joyful sound of a faint baby cry, after which she was quickly transferred to the special care baby unit.

I cried thinking back to Jessica's birth, knowing how much Dan had been looking forward to his first special chat with his new daughter. I had held Grace for a minute before they took her, but Dan didn't even get a cuddle and I was beside myself with worry as the nurses led me down to see my baby girl.

"Please God, let her be OK. Please don't take her from us," I prayed as we reached the doors.

Inside, as I approached my tiny little girl, I saw Dan with his hand through the gap in the incubator and I just caught what he was saying.

"Hi Gracie, I am your daddy my beautiful princess. You gave mummy and me a fright, but everything is going to be OK now, you're going to be OK because I am here for you and I'm going nowhere."

I watched as her tiny little fingers squeezed Dan's and I knew in that instant that we had a little fighter on our hands. She had her Daddy's determination to hold on to love, and I knew she wouldn't let go.

FINDING ME

SO here I am, all grown up!

Married to my best friend, the love of my life, to whom I grow closer, with each passing day. I would never have come this far without him. I would not be the person I am today if it weren't for him, and, above all, I could not be the mummy I had always wanted to be if he weren't by my side.

My life, my heart, my inspiration.

My mum and dad, who I speak to on the phone every single day, continue to be my rocks. They have consistently shown me what it is to be a great parent; to be selfless, compassionate, kind and loving and my daily aim is to be half as good at it, as they are. It is amazing to see how close they are to my children. They teach them things I could never have, and in doing so continue to teach me.

My brother Carl, who went on to meet his birth mother, is happier than ever. Like me, he had a very positive experience with her, and also like me, mum was right there knocking on that big green door with him. He is now in regular contact with his birth mother and her children. Carl has always, and will always be, one of the most important people in my life; and blood or not he is my brother through and through.

Clare, Katherine, Amy and I are still as close as ever. They are my past, my present, and my future. They were at my first birthday party, were standing right up there with me as my bridesmaids on my wedding day and are God-mothers to my children.
Just like we always have been, we always will be best friends.

Mary and I are still very much in contact and I see as much of her as possible. It's not as frequent as when I lived in Dublin, but we both know we are only ever at the other end of the phone. I am so grateful to her for the life she gave me in the past and I'm so grateful to be sharing my future with her.

John and I are no longer in touch. Not all relationships work out the way you would have hoped and I am OK with that. We are two different people on two different paths, but I wish him all the happiness that life can bring.

I have learned so much throughout my journey.

I have learned that life almost never turns out how you expected it to, but if you can find a way to take some good from every experience, you will grow from it. I have learned that the lost little girl I spent so long trying to push away will always be a part of me and that is OK, because she helped make me who I am today. I have learned that when my journey became *our* journey, and I found myself sharing it all with Dan, that everything became that little bit more special and I have learned that, every day my children teach me more than I could ever teach them, and that's a priceless feeling.

These days I no longer have *parts* of my life I am happy with. I am happy with everything I have. As a daughter, a sister, a wife and a mummy I have more than most people dream of; and even though I spent the best part of three decades trying to find myself in a life that might have been, I firmly believe that I didn't.

A better life found me.

Searching for me

"I am searching for me," said a lost little girl,
"Searching for answers to try to understand."
Her mummy, with a tear, looked into her eyes
and tenderly took hold of her hand.

She knows her mummy is there to love her,
she knows her daddy is there to play.
Still, incomplete she needs the answers,
to find her, even just to say...

"I am OK now and I've been adopted,
I would still love to know that you're fine.
You carried me safely and for that I love you,
in my heart, even though you're not mine."

She still looks for the face that looks like hers,
she still wonders how long it will be
until that stranger walks by, sees her face
and just knows...
That lost little girl is me.

by Aoife Curran.